The Spearfisherman's Handbook

The Spearfisherman's Handbook

David Way

ROBERT HALE · LONDON

First published in Great Britain 1981

ISBN 0 7091 8588 X

Robert Hale Limited
Clerkenwell House
Clerkenwell Green
London EC1R 0HT

Photoset by
Kelly Typesetting Limited
Bradford-on-Avon, Wiltshire
Printed in Great Britain by
Lowe and Brydone Ltd., Thetford, Norfolk
Bound by Weatherby Woolnough Ltd., Northants

Contents

For
Thérèse
for so much

Illustrations

PICTURE CREDITS

By courtesy of the *News of the World*, 1; Steve George, jacket, 14, 25; the author, remainder.

Figures

Acknowledgements

No book of this kind could be written without the help of other dedicated spearfishermen and I would like to thank all those who recounted anecdotes and experiences.

The following 'old hands' entrusted me with personal records and photographs or supplied information: Roger Libby, Wally Pack, Mike Davies and Reg Vallintine.

Pete Babbage and Steve George gave up a day's fishing to help with underwater photographs. Photographers Chris Bryan and Paul Aston took great care in processing and printing them.

Thanks are also due to the following: the Hutchinson Publishing Group for permission to quote from Pierre De Latil's classic work *The Underwater Naturalist*; the *News of the World* for allowing me to reproduce (from Roger Libby's collection) the photograph of an early competition sponsored by them; Jacks Sports and Pete Crawford for the loan of equipment; the equipment agents and tourist offices who took the trouble to supply information; the gentlemen of the Ministry of Fisheries and Devon Sea Fisheries Committee at Brixham for the latest rulings on size limits and the staff of the Torquay and Paignton Libraries for their courteous attention.

To my parents, my deepest gratitude for their forbearance with a son who for more than twenty years thought of little else but the bottom of the sea, and to the grandmothers who watched and worried through many a long summer day.

Finally, Tony Rose for helping to fuel an already burning fire of enthusiasm.

INTRODUCTION

In this book I have tried to portray spearfishing in this country as it is today and to give some idea of the exciting possibilities that await those who travel to foreign waters.

During the summer months one meets many enthusiastic, would-be spearfishermen, whose enthusiasm is soon to be dulled by lack of success owing to incorrect equipment, lack of 'field craft', and an assumption that the sea is full of fish waiting to be shot. Spearfishing is not an instant-reward activity, but the rewards arc by no means impossible to obtain. The vast majority of this country's best fishermen are over thirty years of age; if only old heads *could* be put on young shoulders!

It is a mistake to believe, or be led to believe, that spearfishing is merely a snorkel-diving activity which leads to other forms of underwater sport; it is a sport within itself.

To the beginner, the effort and subsequent disappointments at first must seem insurmountable. In British waters we have to contend with cold water, strong tides, and often rough, grey seas of limited underwater visibility.

But gradually, as knowledge is accumulated and the body adapts, the realization dawns that one is succeeding. More fish are seen, their habits understood and whereabouts known at different times of the year and various states of the tide.

Fish are never totally predictable and I make no apology for the many 'ifs', 'maybes' and 'possiblys'; this unpredictability adds to the lure of the sport. One may be hiding in the kelp, watching mullet, when up from the gloom glides a pollack; or a big bass may suddenly appear in the corner of your eye, freezing you with excitement.

When you feel ready and so inclined, competitions may be entered, giving the opportunity to meet fishermen from other parts of the country, thereby increasing your knowledge of equipment and techniques. Regarding competitive fishing, I hope in the space available I have been able to give some long overdue credit to Britain's international teams, whose efforts in a highly demanding sport with all the odds against them, have been largely ignored by their own country's sports media. The story of the international competitions of the last twenty years would fill a book in itself. I would like to think that some day it will be written.

The spearfisherman who learns his art in British waters can feel confident of tackling fish anywhere in the world. Whilst our own fish do not attain the vast dimensions of some overseas species, just as much skill is required in their capture. With spearfishing, man's age-old hunting instinct is satisfied to the full.

Paignton, Devon
1979

1

HISTORY OF THE SPORT

Although a relatively modern sport, spearfishing is by no means a modern occupation. Since the beginning of time men have speared fish for food by standing in boats, wading and diving beneath the waters of rivers, lakes and seas.

It is generally believed that the Polynesians were the first to practise spearfishing in a form similar to the sport we know today. In all probability men were spearing fish in a similar manner throughout the temperate waters of the world as long ago as 100,000 B.C.; that is to say, swimming in sea or river, carrying a pole tipped with bone or flintstone and lunging at whatever fish they chanced upon.

But for all practical purposes, modern spearfishing evolved

Figure 1. Copy of Leonardo Da Vinci's ideas for a snorkel in the sixteenth century. He also designed hand and foot fins

in the south of France in the late 1920s, and its history revolves around the development and continuing improvement of equipment. Man's fishing ability has altered little, if at all, since the pioneering days when young men wearing welders' goggles, clothes-pegs on their noses and armed with two-metre pole spears swam from the coves of Saint Tropez, Cassis, Saint-Jean-Cap-Ferrat, Beauvallon and other beaches along the Riviera. They snatched brief glimpses of bass and mullet, the goggles forced painfully into their eyes by the water pressure. In their spare time they toiled in workshops and smithies improving spears, barbs and constructing prototype guns.

In 1930, a Polynesian javelin champion named Canaque Canaldo speared fish with a triple-headed hand-spear at Marseille. At Cannes in 1934, an American writer and correspondent for the *Saturday Evening Post*, Guy Gilpatric, spearfished with success. In 1938 he wrote *The Complete Goggler*, the first book on the new sport.

Jacques O'Marchal used the first face mask and the first snorkel at La Croix-Valmer in 1927, and exhibited them at the International Nautical Show. There was much experimentation with dental cement, wood, celluloid and, finally, rubber before a Russian named Alec Kramarenko produced a face mask at Nice in 1932. This goggle did not cover the nose, however, and as with the welders' goggles, pressure on the eyes became unbearable at depths of six metres. Bulbs fitted on each side of the goggle allowed a small amount of air to enter, thus easing the pressure on shallow dives. In the same year, also at Nice, Maxime Forjot patented a mask that covered eyes and nose—enabling the wearer to exhale into the mask and equalize the pressure. This is the basic mask we know today.

A Frenchman, Louis De Corlieu, patented his rubber foot-fins in April 1937. An American, Owen Churchill, while in Tahiti, watched boys swimming with home-made fins of soft rubber reinforced with metal strips. On his return to California in 1939 he manufactured under licence, fins of his own design which are still in production today. The sport accelerated in America in much the same way as it had in France ten years before, with the famous San Diego Bottom

Scratchers' Club being formed in 1934. The ranks of spearfishermen were swelled after the war by returning U.D.T. (Underwater Demolition Team) frogmen who continued to use the skills they had acquired on a sporting basis. By 1949 there were 8,000 'gogglers' in southern California alone.

Back in France, June 1938 had seen the patenting of a snorkel tube by Maxime Forjot.

With vision and mobility, all the budding *chasseurs* required were reliable, effective weapons. Georges Beuchat (founder of the firm that bears his name today) had seen Canaldo fishing at Marseille. In 1933 he produced his first 'Tarzan' gun; this *arbalète* working on the crossbow principle was made commercially five years later and is in production to this day. In 1938 also Dr Raymond Pulvenis produced his 'Waterless' rubber-propelled gun. This weapon was unique in that the trigger was on top of the gun and activated by the thumb; wooden versions of this gun, known as 'thumbers' have long been popular with the Tahitians, the world's finest natural spearfishermen. The gun was evolved after experiments with various devices, including a bicycle pump! In 1940, Dr Pulvenis wrote his comprehensive *La Chasse aux Poissons*. Kramarenko favoured a steel spring as the propulsive force for the gun he had patented in 1937 and a year later Forjot also patented a spring gun. With Forjot's gun the spring was extended inside the barrel as opposed to Kramarenko's in which the spring was compressed. The guns were marketed as the 'Fusil Americain' and the 'Douglas'.

Dr Doukan, Henri Broussard, Lt.-Com. Le Prieur and Dr Chénevée were among the men active during this exciting period and were to go on and make their names in the fields of fishing, exploration, archaeology and equipment development. The 1940s were a time of great catches along the Riviera, from Marseille to Nice in particular. Shortage of food during the German Occupation proved a vital incentive for most fishermen and many groupers of 30 kilos with three exceeding 45 kilos were taken. Some fish required a whole day's diving to dislodge them from their caves. In those days before the advent of the wet suit, the bruises and abrasions suffered by the fishermen must have been severe; their physical condition and courage are to be admired.

In 1943, René Cavalero, a French ex-swimming champion, put his soon to become famous Champion *arbalète* on the market. Champion guns were later to win the American Championships for six consecutive years. In 1946 a very significant development occurred in Italy due to the work of the Cressi brothers. The 'Rondine', a full-foot non-cramping fin was marketed after prototypes were made from car-tyre rubber. Two years later they brought out the first low volume mask that enabled the nose to be pinched for equalization. This mask, the 'Pinocchio', and the 'Rondine' fins are still in production today and formed the basic design that many have copied. Almost twenty years were to pass before the next significant fin design appeared—Beuchat's 'Jetfin' which was also widely copied.

One of the first French spearfishing clubs, Le Club des Chasseurs de France, was founded in 1946 by Marcel Isy-Schwart and Jacques Gadreau and was based in Paris. Spanish fishermen formed their first club a year later.

With a knife at his waist, the underwater hunter was now almost fully equipped. The introduction of the dry diving-suit—an Italian wartime development—and later, in the 1950s, the sponge-rubber wet suit, made fishing possible in all climates and throughout the year. There is some doubt as to who actually invented the first wet suits. Frédéric Dumas, an early companion of Cousteau, and leading fisherman of the 1930s, designed a sponge-rubber 'mid-season' jacket, but the first commercially made full-length suit was almost certainly Beuchat's 'Tarzan'. The adoption of neoprene, a synthetic 'sponge-rubber', for the manufacture of wet suits, became universal in the late 1950s and has proved a near perfect material.

Spearfishing, born in the Mediterranean, was now spreading throughout the world.

Adventurous young men in Britain eagerly took to the new sport. At Brighton in 1952, Mike Davies and Bob Charlton formed the Brighton Bottom Scratchers' Club, the first of its kind in Britain, with its H.Q. near the Palace Pier. The club maintained a liaison with Egidio Cressi and a club in the south of France.

The British Sub-Aqua Club was formed in the October of

1953 by the late Peter Small and Oscar Gugen and has grown to become the largest diving club in the world. Bournemouth, one of its first branches (1954) organized the first British Championship; the Bournemouth Club was originally composed entirely of spearfishermen and one of its members, Phil Smith, was Chairman of the B.S-A.C. Sports Committee and instrumental in the organizing of competitions and international teams.

In the summer of 1954 the Looe Underwater Fishing Club was formed and, shortly after, the Plymouth Underwater Fishing Club. Also at Plymouth a group of schoolboys fished together in the Amberjacks Spearfishing Club.

In 1959 the Looe and Plymouth Clubs combined to become The Spearfishing Club of Great Britain, attracting members from all over the country. From that year on into the 1960s, Looe was the venue for the British Championships. In Dorset, the Weymouth Associated Divers' Club produced some of the country's finest international spearfishermen, particularly during the 1960s.

In 1958 the compressed-air powered gun was developed by Nemrod (Spain) and Mares (Italy). Weapons powered by carbon dioxide and explosive cartridges were perfected in France, Italy and the U.S.A.

Breathing Apparatus

In the 1930s and 1940s, the development of the oxygen rebreather and a little later the compressed-air breathing apparatus (aqualung) and their ready use by Mediterranean fishermen resulted in a depletion of territorial fish. In France its use for hunting was banned in 1952 and Spain followed suit shortly after. In Britain there are no government restrictions whatsoever, although the rules of the British Sub-Aqua Club forbid the use of the aqualung for spearfishing, but this does not prevent flat-fish being taken by knife and hand-spear. I, personally, feel no objection to the use of the aqualung for taking big fish in deep water, as is practised in the U.S.A. A fish taken cleanly with an aqualung is preferable to a fish wounded and lost by impossible or inefficient breath-held diving attempts. In point of fact, however, breathing apparatus is of no benefit in our waters with its fish-scaring rumble of bubbles and limited diving duration. Many of us use the aqualung for deeper diving—wrecks, photography and looking-around in the winter months. There are many branches of the British Sub-Aqua Club and Sub-Aqua Association throughout the country who undertake the supervised progressive training the use of the aqualung requires. In this book, we, as spearfishermen, are concerned only in diving with the aid of the simple snorkel tube.

As I write, men are free to fish—as they have for centuries—in almost all the waters of the world. The exceptions are some mid-European countries where opportunity is virtually nil anyway, and conservation areas where scientific bodies and commercial fishing interests have engineered legislation against spearfishermen, forgetting that much of the early knowledge of the natural history of fish was contributed by the sporting fishermen. Far be it from me to decry conservation, but it is often the spearfisherman who is made the scapegoat. The decline of certain species, in certain areas, must not be held up as a typical world-wide example. Fish stocks and the climatic and topographic conditions that govern their capture vary tremendously. Large parts of the British coastline are inaccessible to spearfishermen, being if you like, built-in reserves. The need for conservation—if any—is relative to a certain area and not a world-wide necessity or popular bandwagon to be jumped upon. The minimum weights for fish eligible in B.S-A.C. National Competitions represent larger fish than the size limits governing commercial fishing as laid down by the Ministry of Agriculture and Fisheries. Certain species are banned entirely from competitions (see record list, Appendix II). During the seven competitions of the British National Championship of 1978, a total of 1,501 fish were weighed-in. This does not of course constitute the total number of fish speared throughout the country. But, compared to the number of fish killed in one day by commercial, sporting or industrial activities, the figure of 1,501, or any calculation based upon it, is a mere 'drop in the ocean'. And yet well-known figures in the diving world (many of whom started as spearfishermen) decry our sport without *localized* knowledge. In recent years several diving magazines have waged campaigns against competitive spearfishing in the main and spearfishing in general, but this now appears to be on the wane. Indeed, one leading American publication, for years rather against the sport, has lately been publishing a series containing advice on taking up spear-fishing!

To the seasoned spearfisherman, these staged confrontations can only be somewhat cynically regarded as 'good copy', in rather the same manner as seaside journalists dig out and blow the dust off their 'frogmen speardivers rob crab pots' articles each summer! But these are not matters to concern the beginner. Spearfishing, with its wonderful history behind it and promises of excitement to come, is here to stay. The British spearfisherman can look forward to some of the most consistently good fishing in Europe.

2

EQUIPMENT

It will pay the prospective spearfisherman to take a little time over the choosing of equipment. A well-trained experienced fisherman will catch fish with any old gun, fins and suit, but if quality equipment, designed with breath-held diving in mind, is purchased at the outset, it will pay dividends in comfort and length of time in the water—thus increasing your chances of shooting fish.

Essential: mask, fins, snorkel, wet suit, gloves, knife, weight-belt and fish-keep, float, gun and spares.

Useful: boat, torch, watch, crab or lobster hook, water-tight gear and fish box, knee-pads, set of scales, spare spears, file or piece of sharpening stone.

Below, I list the various items and most suitable models and makes. Unfortunately, some agents do not import a manufacturer's full range, so certain items have to be specially obtained or purchased abroad.[1]

Wherever possible, all items of personal equipment should be inconspicuously coloured so as to avoid detection by wary fish, such as bass. The prices are approximate at the time of writing (autumn 1979).

Masks

Some of the best fishermen have always used the simple, classic round mask, but the trend in recent years has been toward the minimal-volume type for breath-held diving. This type of mask is small and close fitting to the eyes. On diving, the amount of air that has to be blown through the nose into the mask to equalize the pressure of the water is small.

[1] Longo Sub of Italy produce first-class equipment as do many of the accessory manufacturers (spears, spear-heads, reels, etc.) in Italy, France and the U.S.A.

Therefore, the fisherman retains more air in his lungs and increases the time he can stay submerged and the depth he can attain.

Recommended Masks: prices range from £4 to £10.

Lince, Super Lince, Pinocchio, Puma by Cressi of Italy. This firm will grind the glass of these masks to prescription for those with vision problems. Contact the agent in Appendix III.

Micromax by Beuchat of France.

Falco by Technisub of Italy. With this mask the lenses can be replaced by prescription lenses from your optician.

Viso, Ventosa by Mares of Italy.

Equinaut by Champion of France.

Pindos by Spartan of Britain.

Apnea, Aquarius by Pirelli-Ulixes of Italy.

Fins

It has been said that one does not have to be a good swimmer to take up underwater swimming and diving, and whilst this is true, I feel that the prospective spearfisherman, for whom a lot of surface swimming is involved, should be a competent, confident swimmer and not look upon his swim fins as a magical aid, but rather as an extension of his ability. A fin lost in rough water should be an inconvenience, not a disaster.

A large powerful fin is a help in strong tide and for diving deep, quickly. Some types cover the whole foot, others have a foot pocket that comes to the arch of the foot with a strap going behind the heel. Cressi, Sporasub and Mares have been developing plastic and glass-fibre bladed fins. Make sure the fins you choose will fit over hard-soled boots. The heel-strap fin is more suited to large foot sizes.

Recommended Fins: prices range from £12 to £32.

***Jetfin*, ****Super Jetfin* by Beuchat.

***Sporasub Dessault* by Sporasub of France.

****Concord* by Mares.

**Venturi*, ****Competition*, ****Venturi Delphin* by Nemrod of Spain.

****Super Rondine*, ****Rondine Professional* by Cressi.

**Navy Fin* by Champion.

**Giant Continental* by Turnbull of Australia.
**Heel strap*. ***Strap or full foot*. ****Full foot*.

Snorkels
Snorkels should be of the contoured type, curving behind the back of the head. The mask strap is threaded through a holder on the tube. The tube should have a bore diameter of 2½ centimetres. This type of snorkel is vibration free on diving and the large bore gives ease of breathing.
Recommended Snorkels: prices range from £1 to £5.
Big G by Turnbull.
Tubair by Beuchat.
Ghibli by Technisub.
Salou, Irun Professional by Nemrod.
Farallon (mouldable mouthpiece) by Farallon of U.S.A.

Suits
Wet suits are made from neoprene, a synthetic closed cell 'rubber' composed of bubbles of nitrogen. A small amount of water (about half a litre) seeps in and warms to body temperature. The thicker the material of the suit, the warmer it will be, but thick (8 mm) material can restrict the freedom of movement necessary when fishing.

The spearfisherman generally spends long periods in the water, so the ordinary off-the-peg four-piece suit with zips that let in water does not give adequate protection from the cold—certainly not if six-hour competitions are contemplated. The jacket should be in one piece, the hood being attached, and it should have no zips, except possibly one at the front, about one metre long running down from the breast to close between the jock-strap fasteners. The material of the hood should come to just above the eyes and under the bottom lip. The forehead is particularly vulnerable to cold as is the nape of the neck, so make sure the whole hood is a snug fit (but not too tight as the water must have access to the ears, as explained in Chapter 4). The chest part of the suit can be a little on the loose side to allow for maximum chest expansion. When dressing, the waist is turned up and the jacket pulled on like a sweater. For those who are a little, can I say, overweight, this type of jacket, even with a short zip, may prove difficult to get into. In this case, a hood-attached jacket with a zip running from between the jock-strap fasteners at the bottom edge right up to the side of the cheek may prove easier. This style will not be quite as warm as a zipless jacket, but much better than the separate hood type since there is no point of entry for water at the important neck area.

'Long John' type trousers that come up to the shoulder, help insulate the trunk of the body. To make dressing easier, a zip running down from below the neck or a velcro fastening on one of the shoulder straps can be fitted. For winter or early season fishing, a 3- or 4-mm neoprene undervest worn under the 'Long John' can be a welcome accessory. The suit is completed by a pair of hard-soled boots—the ordinary sock-type bootees wear out in no time and are hopeless for walking any distance. Expensive boots, by a good manufacturer, are cheapest in the long run. The soles of cheap boots fall off after a short time and although half the price, only last a quarter of the time. To prevent wear on the knees of the suit, knee-patches can be fitted or pads can be made from scraps of neoprene (see inset Fig. 25).

Most suit manufacturers tend to make stock sizes only, with coloured tapes and hoods—not much help if you are trying to surprise a bass! Cressi and Beuchat make excellent suits, as do Mares, but they are not cheap. Most of us go to a small suitmaker, perhaps a fellow diver, where the garment can be made to your exact measurements and specification. It is not too difficult to make your own if you buy a kit from a good dive shop or one of the firms that advertise in the diving Press, but make sure that they understand the style of suit that you require. The cheapest way is to make the entire suit yourself from sheets of neoprene, but get experienced advice before attempting this.

The type of material is not critical but the thickness should be at least 4 mm. Four-mm trousers and 6-mm jacket is a good comfortable combination. Neoprene is available in many surface and interior finishes: shark skin, turtle skin, smooth skin and nylon both sides (double-lined). Double-lined has the advantage that both sides of the seam can be sewn. If you choose it, make sure it is of good quality as some linings come away from the neoprene after a while in the form of large blisters.

Nylon inner linings can be plain or towelling. Most fishermen prefer a plain lining (towelling takes a longer time to dry). Some swear by an unlined suit although the bare neoprene is difficult to get on and off, requiring the use of talcum powder or french chalk as a lubricant, however, their advocates swear they are warmer because the suit contains less water. It is widely believed that shark or turtle skin wears better than smooth skin, but it is my experience that a suit gets chipped and scraped whatever the finish—smooth, stippled or lined.

Tape covering of the seams is unnecessary providing the suit is well glued and *correctly* stitched. Make sure your suit is stitched on the inside only (unless double-lined), not right through the material since that allows the water your body has warmed to seep out, being replaced by fresh, cold water. A well-made and fitted suit will give protection in water of 40°F, below that, extreme enthusiasm is required!

Expect to pay at least £60 for a kit suit and £100 for a ready-made one.

Gloves

Several kinds, in thin neoprene, are available. The black nylon both sides type is best. During the summer, gardening gloves can be used.

Knives

A knife is an essential item and must always be carried. Killing and cleaning fish and cutting snagged line are its main uses. An endless variety is available on the market, but the majority are intended for heavy diving work. I suggest that you go for the narrow-bladed, stiletto type. Most fishermen, myself included, use a ground-down kitchen or vegetable knife.

The knife is worn on the calf, thigh, arm, or weight-belt. Make sure the handle is secured to the sheath—a piece of inner tubing is ideal—but not so tightly that it cannot be quickly withdrawn.

Weight-Belt

The weighted belt counteracts the fisherman's buoyancy. Any belt with a *foolproof quick release* that can be operated in a single, one-handed movement is suitable. The 'H' type weights stay in position on the belt better than the slotted variety. The lead weights can be bought, but it is possible to make your own, either with a wood or plaster of Paris mould. Weight moulds are also available from dive shops. Cast them in 1½, 1 and ½ kilo sizes. The amount of ballast required varies with the individual and can be anything from 4 kilos to 8 kilos, or more. Adjust the buckles so that the belt fits quite tightly—to allow for compression of the suit when diving. If the belt is too loose, it will slide up and down on diving and surfacing. Put enough weights on the belt to enable you to lie still on the bottom in three metres of water but be careful not to overweight—making surface swimming difficult.

Some fishermen (among them several times Channel Islands Champion Mike Holt, Mike Bradshaw and the majority of the Jersey fishermen) use the French type of belt known as a *baudrier*. It comprises a waist belt and weights with a large back weight; shoulder straps connecting the large weight to the waist belt (Fig. 27A). Although not widely used, a *baudrier* tends to distribute the weight more comfortably.

Fish-Keep

It would be inconvenient to have to return to shore each time a fish is caught, so the fish has to be carried on the fisherman's person. This is achieved by means of a 'fish-keep', sometimes called a 'stringer'. Take a piece of stainless steel or brass about 14 cm long and 2 cm wide. Drill a hole of 3 mm diameter at one end and grind the other to a point. Just back from the point make as large an oblong hole as possible. Attach a piece of 3 mm braided nylon line to the blunt end and at the other end of the line make a loop. The piece of line should be about 30 cm long. Tie a dog-lead clip to one end of your weight-belt, at the other end a large stainless steel snap-hook, like the kind obtainable in yachting stores and called a *carabini* or a carbine hook. The loop at the end of the line is attached to the small clip and the oblong hole in the piece of metal hooked onto the big clip. The piece of line runs across the fisherman's waist

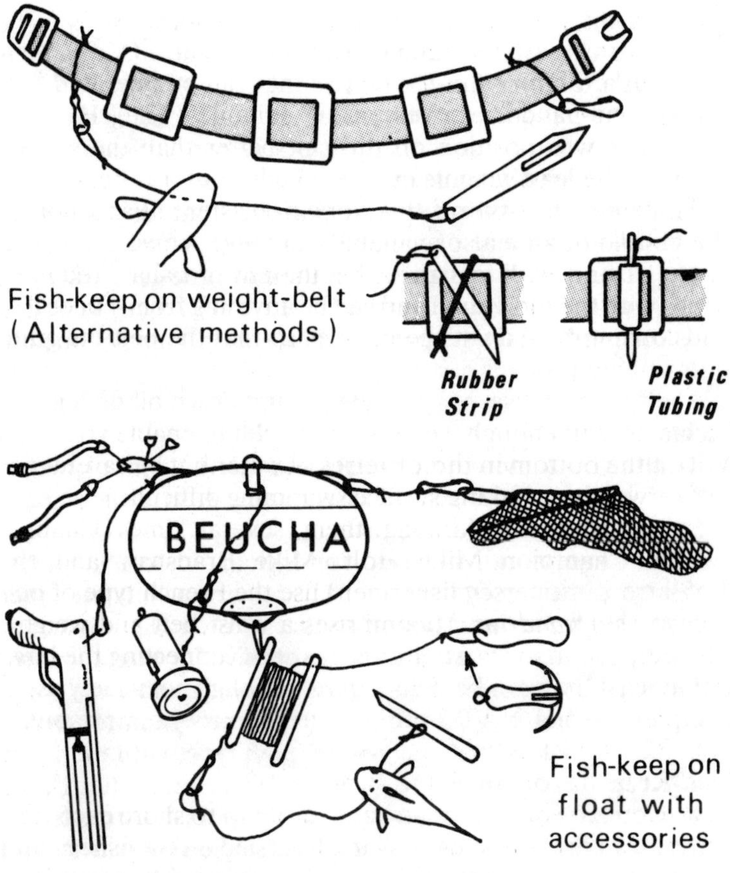

Figure 2. Accessories for weight-belt and float

when the belt is in position. I might add, here, that it is surprising the number of fish that can be carried on a 30-cm length of line. Some men thread the line through a piece of plastic tubing to make it more rigid and easier to handle in the water.

When a fish has been speared—and whilst it is still on the spear—kill it by putting the pointed end of the keep under the gill covers and breaking the spine. Thread the fish by pushing the keep straight through its eyes, clip up the keep and the fish will hang behind your back and out of the way. Instead of securing the piece of metal to a clip, an alternative is to tie some strong elastic around one of the weights. The metal is then pushed under the elastic to secure (Fig. 2, top). While not as secure as a clip, it eliminates any rattle during diving—important when after wary fish in still conditions as often found in the Mediterranean.

To make a fish-keep for attaching to a float, drill a hole in the middle of a piece of metal 21 cm long. Attach a piece of ½-metre line, with a small loop at the end. The keep will hang from your float like an inverted 'T'. Fish are killed, threaded and come up against the piece of metal at right-angles and are thus retained.

Floats

With the yearly increase of boats and skiers, a float (surface marker buoy) is an essential safety item. Also, fish, a spare spear and a net can be hung from it.

Many objects can be used for a float—mooring buoys, 4.55-litre plastic containers, footballs, or an inflated inner tube folded in half and bound so that it resembles a banana. The purpose-made floats are very expensive for what they are, but at least they can be deflated for travelling and some come complete with a NATO 4 diving flat or provision for fitting one. The Beuchat float is a good, tough type, with the inner bladder being contained in a strong outer cover. Although the new torpedo-shaped floats are easily pulled through the water, they are unfortunately made of single skin plastic, and so can puncture with rough use. The most visible colour is flame orange.

To the bottom of the float attach an 'H'-shaped winder holding 20 metres or so of braided nylon or courlene line. Sufficient line is unwound, dependent on depth, then clipped or secured in a notch on the winder. At the end of the line tie a lead weight of about 500 grammes. About 3 metres back from the weight fix a small cork which will prevent the line entangling you. Some fishermen put another cork at about 6 metres to keep the rest of the line floating and out of the way. The weight is held in the hand to tow the float and dropped to moor it. For areas with strong tides, such as Selsey Bill, Sussex, a grapnel will moor the float securely, whereas a weight can drag.

Torches

A torch is useful when fishing for conger or pouting—fish that live in dark caves and recesses. The torch should have a switch that can be easily manipulated by the thumb.

The six-cell Mares *Novalux*, Cressi *Tana*, Technisub *Orion* and G.S.D. *Samantha* are good examples.

Watches

A must for competitions where time is vital. Buy the best you can afford, avoiding those with more than one winder—the winder being the potential leakage point. A bezel and luminous hands are the only justifiable refinements. Wear the watch under the cuff of your suit to prevent line snagging on it, or the crystal getting scratched. A nylon webbing strap passing through both attachments is safer and everlasting compared with 'tropic' straps that soon crack.

Guns

Owing to the diversity of weapons available today, I have left the subject of guns until last. The merits of each type are strongly upheld by their adherents and among the leading makes there is little to choose regarding power, accuracy and quality.

The vast majority of guns on the British market are of Italian, French or Spanish manufacture and consequently they reflect the Mediterranean style of fishing. The most sought-after fish in the Mediterranean has always been the grouper, a sedentary, cave-living fish, generally taken at close range. Therefore, short, powerful, easily manoeuvred guns gained prominence. The longer 'open water' guns are more suited to our British style of fishing—the exceptions being for use against conger; fishing in holes and under ledges and for flat-fish and fishing in waters of poor underwater visibility, where a shorter weapon is a great advantage.

For all practical purposes there are three methods of spear propulsion used for today's guns: steel spring, compressed air and rubber bands.

SPRING-POWERED. Spring-powered guns are rarely seen today, of the great spring guns of the past, to my knowledge,

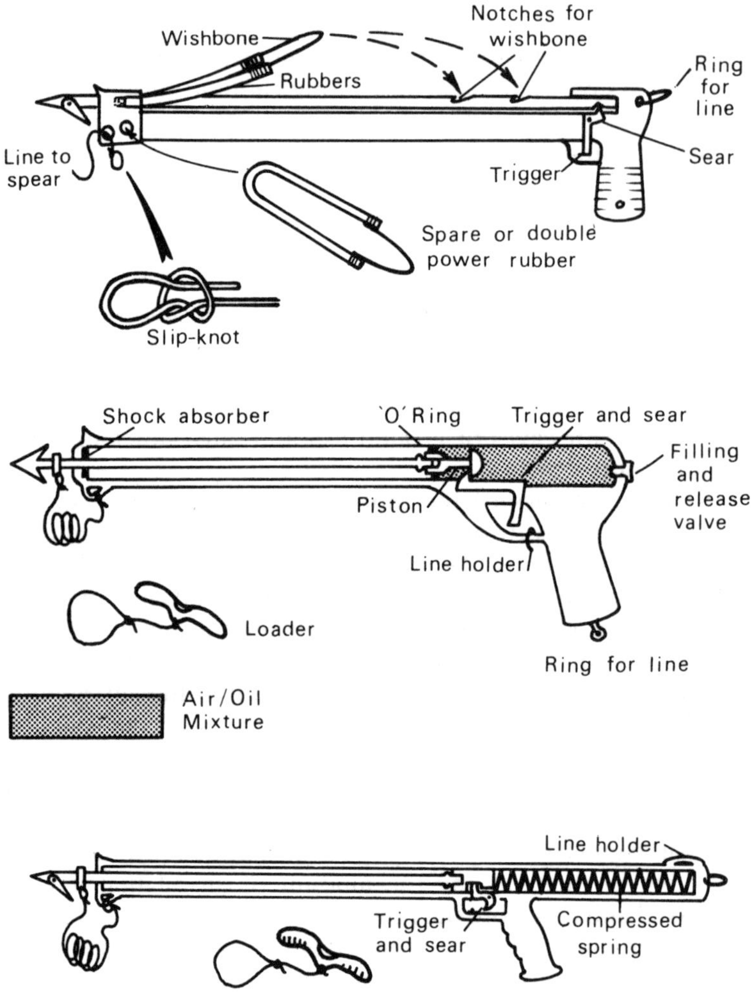

Figure 3. Basic construction and operation of the three main types of gun

only two are still being manufactured—the Cressi 'Saetta' and Mares 'Bess'. Although powerful and accurate, they tend to throw a slow shaft, and the spring, housed inside the long barrel, requires regular attention against corrosion and sand particles, and weakens with a lot of use.

COMPRESSED-AIR/OIL POWERED. Compressed-air guns were developed by Nemrod in Spain during the early '50s and are widely used in Great Britain. Their main features are: good power-to-length ratio; clean lines, allowing quick tracking movements; a generally rugged construction; the latest rear-handled models float—a great advantage; some models have a variable power switch, i.e. 'low' for loading, 'medium' for caves or ground fish and 'high' for long, open water shots.

The mechanics of the modern air-gun are quite simple. Basically, the body of the gun is a tube, inside which runs the barrel. The tube is filled with a measure of low viscosity oil then with the pump supplied, air is pumped into the tube. Running inside the barrel is a piston and the end of the spear shaft fits into the piston which is then pushed down the barrel—thus compressing the air and oil in the surrounding tube. The piston connects with the trigger sear and is held in check. When the trigger is pulled the expanding air/oil forces the piston along until it comes up against a shock absorber at the end of the barrel, the spear continues on its way.

Some guns have a power regulator that seals off sections of the barrel thus varying the amount of air/oil that is compressed and therefore the power. With guns that do not have a power regulator, air can be added or released prior to entering the water thus giving a 'hard' or 'soft' shot. A loader, supplied with the gun, fits over the spear point allowing it to be rammed down the barrel for loading. Tie a strip of rubber with a loop to the loader, put the loop over your wrist and tuck the loader up your suit cuff. Guns with a power regulator can be loaded with the bare hand, the switch in the 'low' position. Some models have a centre hand grip with the air chamber behind it, others a rear grip with the chamber forming part of the barrel. This latter type is gaining in popularity owing to its lightness and manoeuvrability.

Spear shafts are in 7, 8 or 9-mm diameters, the ends threaded so that damaged heads can be replaced. Spears are usually supplied with a twin-barbed head, but a variety of head designs are available (Fig. 4). For fast fish in poor visibility, some men fit three-, four- or five-tined heads to increase the chance of a hit. Take careful note of the instructions supplied with an air-gun.

Recommended models: prices range from £35 to £140 according to size.

MARES. *Supersten 100* and *130, Sten, Medisten and Ministen, Miniministen*: a handy, well-made gun, in six lengths—130 cm, 100 cm, 90 cm, 70 cm, 58 cm and 41 cm. A floating gun, the grip is at the rear. Two-position power regulator on Sten and Medisten. *Mirage*: similar in function to the Stens. Adjustable power regulator, 80-cm length only. *Vicojet*: larger than the Stens, made in two sizes—De-Luxe (120 cm), Tana (90 cm). Handle is in the middle of the gun, with the air chamber behind it. Although an excellent gun, not as adaptable as the Stens for British fishing. *Bazooka*: 140 cm. Very powerful gun for sharks and fish of over 30 kilos.

CRESSI. *Superleggero*: well-made popular gun in four lengths—40 cm and 55 cm without power regulator; 70 cm and 95 cm with or without power regulator. *Mach and Jumbo*: beautifully made guns, mid-mounted grips; the Jumbo has a two-position power regulator. Mach in two sizes—90 cm, and 110 cm. Jumbo in three—100 cm, Mini Jumbo 81 cm, Micro Jumbo 62 cm.

TECHNISUB. *Fucile Jeans*: easy to dismantle with ordinary tools. Rear-handled, in three lengths—55 (600 mm), 70 (750 mm), 85 (900 mm).

G.S.D. Attractive Italian guns with unique, simplified piston and internal mechanisms. *Katiuscia*: Rear grip with handy three-position power regulator at rear of barrel, 80 cm. Manufacturers claim 15 per cent more power when pumped to comparable pressures. *Gran Gara*: same features as the Katiuscia but with centre hand grip and smaller diameter barrel, 83 and 110 cm. *Dynamic*: Shorter versions of the Katiuscia, 28 and 53 cm.

COPINO. A very well-engineered Spanish gun, in various

sizes. I do not know of a supplier in this country. Widely sold in Spain and used by some of their top fishermen.

NEMROD. One of the pioneers of the compressed-air gun, they ceased production of their best guns—Fragata and Corbeta—in the '60s. Present range is extensive. *Dragon*: 118 and 89 cm. *Clipper*: 47, 68, 89 and 123 cm. All have the mid-position hand grip.

RUBBER POWERED. Rubber-powered guns are very popular in France, America and Australia. They have some devout users in Britain, myself included. The simplicity of the *arbalète* means total reliability. The spear lies on top of an air-tight alloy tube or wooden barrel, at one end of which is the handle and trigger mechanism. At the forward end is the 'head', into which two rubber strands are screwed.

Some guns have a hole through which one longer rubber is threaded, thus providing a spare or extra power. This rubber is know as a wrap-around rubber. The loose ends of the rubbers are connected by a 'V'-shaped piece of wire called the 'wishbone'. The rubbers are pulled along the top of the spear shaft and the wishbone hooked into a notch just in front of the trigger mechanism—into which the end of the spear shaft has been locked. On pulling the trigger, the rubbers contract and throw the spear.

The rubber gun owes its origins to the natives of Polynesia and was brought to its present stages of development by Georges Beuchat and René Cavalero of Marseille.

Rubbers are available in various thicknesses and power, and although they can, with a lot of use, break or lose some of their power, they are easily replaced. Spares can be carried on a float or around the neck. Spears supplied are 7-mm twin-barbed or 5 or 6-mm Tahitian single-barbed where spear-head and shaft are in one piece and it is not possible to unscrew the head. The 'thin' Tahitian spear has a number of advantages: the small diameter does little damage to the fish, making a sometimes invisible hole; the light weight (around 400 grammes) makes for a fast flight (even faster if the standard nylon line is replaced by thick nylon monofilament), and if a fish is lightly hit it will not pull out as easily as a heavy shaft;

fish removal is quick—the shaft is turned and the barb falls closed, allowing the fish to be slipped off.

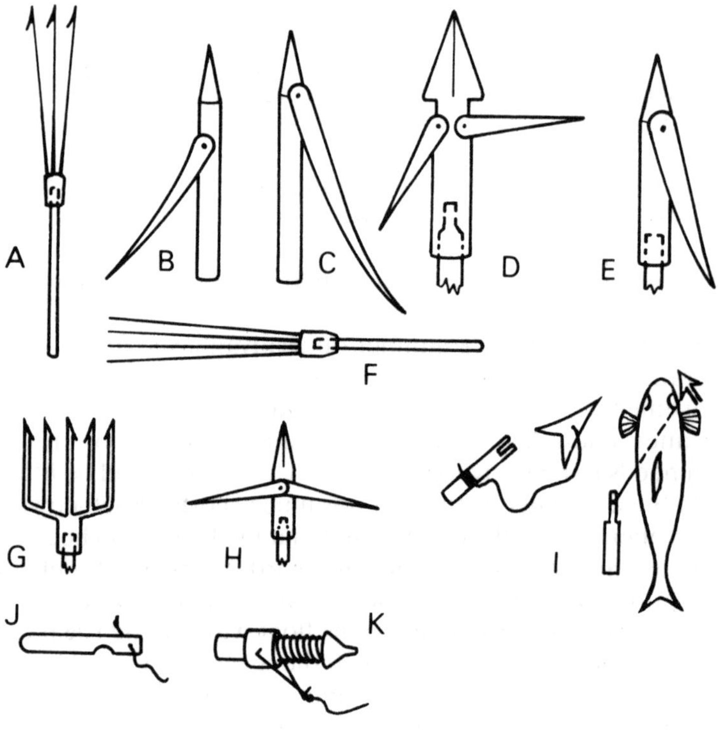

Figure 4. **Types of spear-head.** (Not drawn to scale) A. Barbed spronger. B. 5 or 6 mm Tahitian. C. Tahitian with extra long 'flopper' barb. D. Heavy-duty twin-barb for 8 or 9 mm shaft. E. Single barb for 8 or 9 mm shaft. F. Australian-type barbless spronger. G. Five-tined head. H. Twin-barb for 8 or 9 mm shaft. I. American 'slip tip' detachable head for very large fish, with stainless steel cable and detachable head in operation. J. Tahitian spear line attachment. K. Sliding ring and shock-absorbing spring for 8 or 9 mm shaft.

Some men fit a spear-head known as a 'spronger', a copy of a spear-head used by the native fishermen of the Pacific. A spronger has a large hitting area like a five-tined head and the fish is held by extended flexion with little chance to move. Removal of the fish is simplified on the barbless type. Popular in Australia, a spronger in a home-made wooden gun was used by the well-known film maker, Ron Taylor, to take a 50-kilo Napolean fish during the last minutes of the 1965 World Championship, and gave him victory. For very large fish, a detachable head is used. The spear-head fits in a ferrule or slot and is attached to the shaft by a short length of steel cable. On penetration the head comes loose so the fish cannot break the barbs or lever itself off the spear.

Two notches are cut on spear shafts giving a choice of power. When powerful rubbers are being used, it is easier to load by pulling to the first notch, taking a rest, then pulling to the second notch.

Rubber guns have a number of disadvantages: the rubbers vibrate when the gun is moved quickly toward a fish and movements are not as smooth as with an air-gun, with its 'cleaner' lines. Also, in order to obtain maximum power, the gun needs to be fairly long (around 1.75 metres) and be fitted with thick rubbers. If the gun was much shorter, such powerful rubbers would have to be used that loading would become difficult. So it can be seen that as regards the power-to-length ratio, the air-gun is superior—storing more energy in a smaller weapon. All rubber guns float without the spear, so both hands are free to take fish off the spear. They are cheaper to manufacture than air-guns and consequently cheaper to buy being about half the cost of an air-gun.

The prospective fisherman must consider a number of points when choosing a gun. Firstly, the area in which he intends to do most of his fishing. If visibility is nearly always poor (1–2 metres) a short, manoeuvrable gun is the answer. The Sussex coast is a good example; fishing is in wrecks or among the few patches of boulder or other available cover and shots have to be quick. Also, a lot of 'bottom' fishing is practised for fish such as plaice, sole, skate and conger.

On the other hand, the fisherman in clear water, such as the South-West, (where the summer visibility can be 4 metres and as much as 20 metres in certain areas), needs a longer, more accurate gun for shots of greater distance. The longer the barrel the greater the accuracy—the spear being guided for a greater part of its journey. The obvious answer is two guns of a medium length, variable power air-gun. so that you are prepared for all conditions, all around the coast.

The effective range of a gun depends on its length and the amount of energy it can store. A rubber or air-gun of 130 cm length should be able to transfix a kilo fish at a distance of 2½ metres. Competition rubber guns with two 1½-cm diameter slings and a 6-mm spear with a thin line, have been effective to 6 metres. All guns have a safety-catch that locks the trigger.

Recommended models: prices range from £15 to £40, according to size.

BEUCHAT. Ten models up to 135 cm in length. The silver-barrelled *Caraibe Competition* is an ideal gun for open water fishing for mullet and bass with the 5 or 6 mm Tahitian 'thin' spear. *Marlin*: new model with a number of refinements—sensitive, adjustable trigger pull, new safety-catch and hand grip.

CHAMPION. Very similar to the Beuchat, only the sear and trigger mechanism differ. Sixteen models—*Junior* to *Luxe*. *Canon* has pad extension behind butt for comfortable loading. Choice of 6, 7, 8 or 9-mm spears.

DESSAULT. Made by Sporasub of Marseille. A first-class gun with advanced trigger mechanism. Made in fifteen models, but only popular lengths imported.

TECHNISUB. Extensive range. Six guns with attractive Australian style wooden barrels. Lengths—110 cm to 142 cm. Double rubbers on the larger guns—*Cave Master Special, Bazooka Special and Clubman Special. Zip*: Five models with metal barrels, 88 cm to 138 cm. Double rubbers on three guns. All Technisub rubber guns have an extension loading pad.

CRESSI. *Australia*: Three models with choice of 6 or 7 mm Tahitian spear.

An advantage of these five rubber-powered guns is that all rubbers, wishbones and spears are interchangeable—simplifying the problem of spares.

When it comes to purchasing a gun, it is not simply a matter of strolling into the nearest sports or dive shop and seeing all the guns I have described on display. Most sports-shops owners—and I am afraid some dive-shop owners—have never heard of some of the better guns. Do not be talked into buying one of the 'holiday-maker's' guns so often seen on display! Contact the agents at the end of the book or get advice from an experienced fisherman if your local shop has a poor selection.

Other Types of Guns and Spear-heads

The three types of guns that I have described are the most practical. The largest and most powerful models are capable of taking—with the right techniques—fish of several hundred kilos. Other methods of spear propulsion are by compressed CO_2 and explosive cartridge.

Carbon dioxide guns, known in America as gas guns, were popular there in the 1950s. Some had evocative names like 'Manta' and 'Thunderbolt' and could be fitted with 'Jet Fire' and 'Thunderhead' powerheads. They use a cylinder of compressed carbon dioxide, as used on a soda syphon or similar, to drive the spear out of the barrel. They have tremendous penetrative power, but each time the spear is fired, the cylinder has to be replaced. They are similar in appearance to the mid-handled compressed-air guns. Pelletier of Paris have long been a leading manufacturer of CO_2 guns and Farallon of the U.S.A. make anti-shark heads ('shark darts'). Cartridge guns are precision-made firearms powered by a blank cartridge. The cartridge (usually .22) is inserted in the breech as in a bolt action rifle. On firing, the explosion drives the spear from the barrel, giving, it is claimed, great power and accuracy. A supply of cartridges has, of course, to be carried. The American Tapmatic Corporation's 'SMG' is the best example.

Neither CO_2 or cartridge guns are permitted in national or international competitions where the gun must be loaded by the muscular effort of the competitor (see rule 6, Chapter 7). Some countries have laws restricting or prohibiting the use of expellable gas weapons.

The spears of these 'elephant guns' (or any gun) can be fitted with the usual barbed head or a powerhead. A power-head screws onto the end of the spear shaft or fits onto the spear head and is composed of a chamber containing a spring-loaded firing pin held in check by a safety-pin, and a spear-head. A cartridge (.22 or 303) is placed in the chamber and the pin cocked. On impact, the pin detonates the cartridge, pushing the spear-head well into the fish.

A variation is a larger chamber containing a waterproof 20- to 12-gauge cartridge loaded with BB or SG shot, but no spear-head. On impact the cartridge fires and the fish is literally 'shot'. Most leading manufacturers include several types of powerhead in their ranges for guns or hand-spears. Owing to the fact that powerheads have to be cocked and fire on impact, they are extremely dangerous in irresponsible hands. Their main use is as a defence against sharks.

The expense and inconvenience of CO_2, cartridge guns and powerheads makes them specialized weapons and of little use in British waters where in almost every case it would be the same as using a deer rifle for a pigeon.

The Law Relating to Spearguns

In past times there was some doubt as to whether possession of a speargun required a shot-gun and/or a firearm certificate. After consulting the police and an established dive-shop owner who is also a firearms dealer, it appears that the rubber, compressed-air and spring guns at present being imported into this country do not require a licence.

The question of CO_2, cartridge guns and powerheads is a little more complex because things such as barrel length, type of bore, i.e. smooth or rifled, have to be considered. So, if one intends to import or even make a weapon of this type, the official advice is consult the police. Penalties for breach of firearms laws are heavy.

The tolerant attitude of the British authorities towards spearguns is due, I am sure, to the almost non-existent number of injuries. I personally know of only two cases; both self-inflicted due to careless loading whilst in the water.

If we regard all guns and spears as *potentially lethal and handle them accordingly*, we should have no fear of legislation. Never fire a gun on land; without the cushioning effect of the water the gun can be seriously damaged.

Hand-Spears

A simple hand-spear is often sufficient for flat-fish. A broom handle or bamboo pole, two metres long with a piece of sharp,

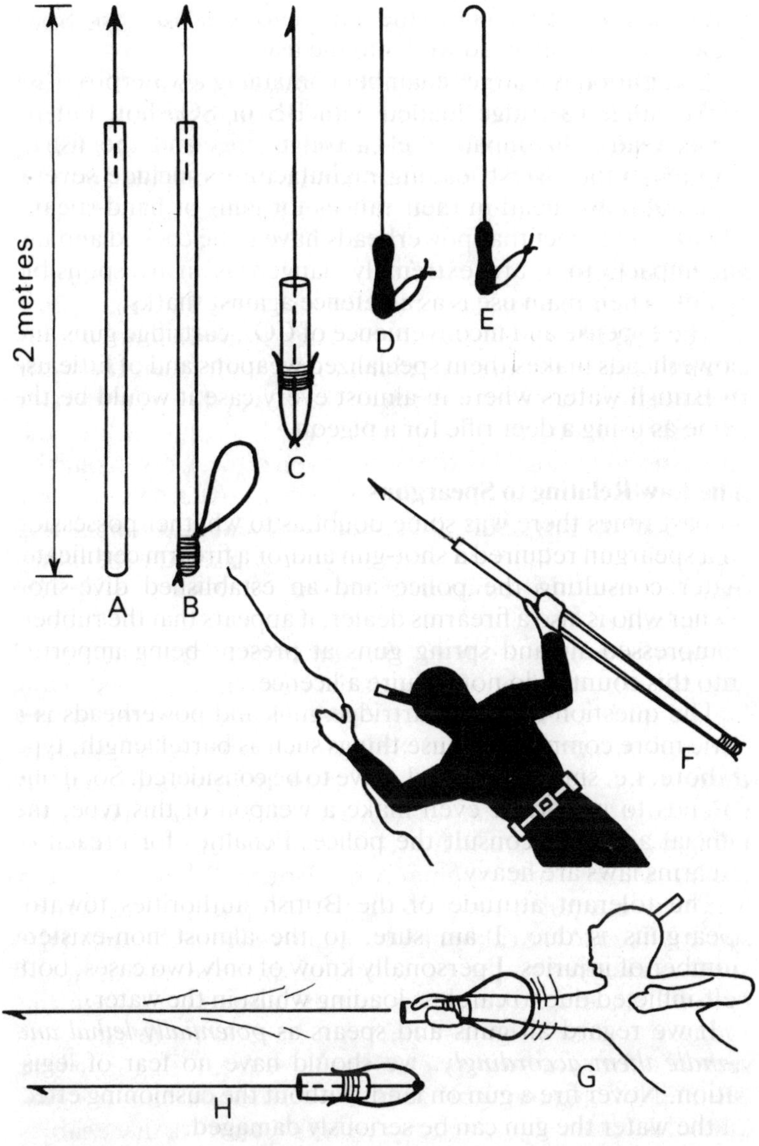

Figure 5. A. Simple pole spear. B. Pole spear with rubber sling. C. Hawaiian sling. D. Short hand-spear with wrist lanyard. E. Crab or lobster hook. F. Sling pole spear ready to fire. G. Firing position of Hawaiian sling. H. Captive Hawaiian sling

barbed 6 mm steel rod fixed securely into the end is the basic idea.

A further development is a thick catapult elastic sling tied to the end of the pole. Put your hand through the loop so that it lies under the thumb and across the back of the hand. Stretching the elastic, run your hand along the pole and grip it; on releasing your grip the pole flies forward.

Hawaiian Sling

Another simple spear, popular abroad, is the Hawaiian sling. Take a bamboo or plastic tube and tightly bind a loop of thick catapult elastic or surgical tubing to one end. Insert the spear through the other end; a notch on the end of the spear fits over the rubber loop. Grip loop and spear and pull back to the chin, straightening the other arm as you do so. Look along the outstretched arm and release the spear. Alternatively, for one-handed firing, pull the elastic back and grip rubber and spear just behind the tube; release your grip and the spear flies out. The end of the two-metre, 6- or 7-mm spear is usually single barbed.

Spearfishermen from Florida have had great success in international competitions with their simple 'shooters'. Don Del Monico took a 22-kilo grouper during the 1961 World Championships at Almeria, Spain to help the U.S.A. team to third place. He was placed third in the previous year at Palermo, Italy. A great athlete, Del Monico also has a 345-kilo grouper to his credit from his home waters. A variation of the Hawaiian sling popular with British fishermen is the 'Captive' Hawaiian sling. With this weapon the end of the spear is fixed to the rubber loop, so that on firing the end of the spear is checked at the beginning of the tube and does not actually leave the tube. This has the advantage that in the event of a miss the spear does not have to be retrieved or searched for. The secret of landing large fish with a sling is in 'stoning' (killing outright) the fish with the first shot. It is this kind of accurate shooting coupled with teamwork that enables men like the Pinder brothers and Del Monico to take their large fish. A fish of 4 kilos can easily carry the spear away with it, if hit in a non-vital part of its body. But in often murky British waters, variations of the hand-spear are often useless for fast moving round fish that appear, and are gone, in a flash; although I remember four or five years ago Roger Libby of Plymouth, a long-serving fisherman, taking a bass with a sling. A very creditable achievement bearing in mind this species' speed and alertness.

All items of equipment will last longer if given a rinse in fresh water after use. Take care to remove sand from the barrels and trigger areas of guns. Spear points should be kept sharp and the barbs oiled so they swing open freely. Keep a supply of spares—mask and fin straps, rubbers, wishbones and fish keeps.

The reader may be wondering about the price of all this equipment. It is difficult to state a price for a particular item these days as discounts and offers vary from store to store—a mask for example may vary by as much as £2. Good second-hand equipment can often be had—especially guns; but satisfy yourself that fins or a mask really fit and have no signs of perishing—always check the sealing edge of a mask. To outfit yourself for spearfishing will cost from £150 to £200—possibly a little less if you 'shop around'.

Equipment Containers

For travelling, a cloth or canvas case can be made up to carry your gun and spears securely and safely. Suit and fins, can be packed in a kit-bag available from government surplus stores, or you can buy one of the P.V.C. bags or grips from a dive shop.

A plastic dustbin or box in the boot of your car will prevent the water draining from gear and fish causing rust and odour problems. A boot smelling of fish may be a source of satisfaction to fishermen, but other members of the family do not seem to appreciate it in the same way!

3

BOATS

A boat can be of immense help to the spearfisherman, increasing his chances of success and saving a lot of time and effort otherwise spent on swimming. Large areas of coastline can be visited until fish or better conditions are found. One can, of course, operate from any kind of boat, but if it is intended to purchase a boat specifically for spearfishing, there are three types ideally suited: the small fibreglass or wooden **motor boat,** known as a fishing or day boat—converted life-boats are good examples; the **dory** in fibreglass and, more rarely, aluminium or wood; the **inflatable dinghy** in reinforced neoprene.

I shall discuss each type of boat with its advantages and disadvantages.

Fishing Boats

This boat in 4 to 6 metres length is to me a near ideal vessel. Its advantages are: comfort, especially if a cuddy or cabin is fitted; economical running and initial purchase costs; one can dress on board and food and drink can be carried; stability when climbing in or out.

This type of boat, if strongly constructed in wood and properly looked after, will virtually last forever. Do not confuse the seagoing type, which will take seas of up to Force 6 in relative comfort with the thin-planked, narrow-ribbed estuary or river variety. If you are lucky and look around, it is possible to obtain a fishing boat complete with inboard engine for £350–£500. Type of engine is not particularly important, though several points are worth considering. Diesel engines are less complex, more reliable and with the increasing cost of fuel, much cheaper to run. Their almost total acceptance by professional fishermen speaks for itself.

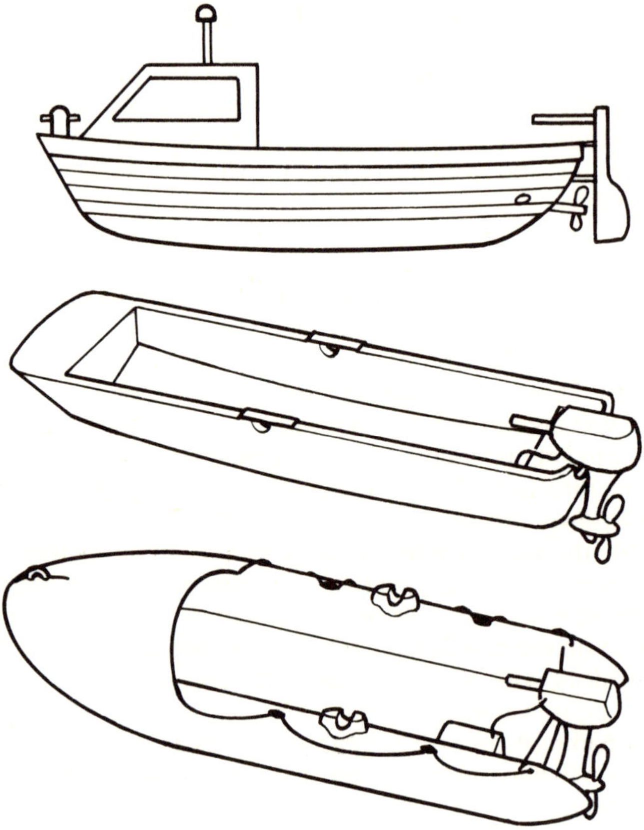

Figure 6. *Top to bottom*: fishing boat, dory, inflatable

This type of boat has three big disadvantages. Unless the vessel is small and light, it will have to be kept on a permanent mooring. If you live by the sea in a good fishing area, this is no problem, although moorings can be expensive and of limited availability in certain harbours. If you live inland or wish to travel to various parts of the country, you will have to choose a small vessel of this type or a dory or inflatable that can be towed and subsequently easily launched.

In the event of a breakdown or for an overhaul, an inboard engine cannot simply be unclamped and taken away. Work has to be done on site and this can be inconvenient and costly.

Although of course an outboard engine can be used on this type of boat and, indeed, the fitting, near the stern, of a bracket to take a spare 'wing' engine is a wise precaution in the event of a breakdown on the main engine while at sea.

Owing to hull design this type of boat is slow through the water and will not compete with the slowest dory or inflatable.

Dories

Dories have a good reputation for stability (more so with a 'cathedral' hull), speed and plenty of space. Their shallow draught allows manoeuvring over reefs and close to rocky coasts. They are capable of carrying heavy loads—a 4-metre dory will take four fishermen with gear and fish in comfort. In order to get maximum speed with the boat on the 'plane', that is the hull just clear of the water, an engine of at least 20 horsepower is required.

One disadvantage of a dory is exposure to the elements, felt the more so late and early in the season when a couple of hours in a wet, wet suit can be uncomfortable. A 'dodger' or screen on the bow is a great help in cutting down spray. Look for a dory with a fair amount of freeboard, i.e. depth from gunwale to waterline.

In comparison with inflatables, dories are heavy. This is no problem when the trailer can be taken down a slipway and the boat floated off. When launching from a beach it will take four men to carry a 4-metre dory any distance. Otherwise, it will have to be dragged but this can damage the hull unless rollers are used.

With all fibreglass boats any damage to the gel coat or outer skin must be made good, otherwise water will seep in, gradually saturating the porous fibres, thus making the boat increasingly heavy. In time it will start to disintegrate. Fibreglass is not the everlasting, maintenance-free material one is inclined to believe.

Dories vary in price according to specification. A bare 4-metre hull can be bought for £200 upwards. Seats, controls and mountings you fit yourself, or, of course, buy complete for around £600.

The *Fishing News*, a paper for professional fishermen,

carries plenty of advertisements for boats of all types. Occasionally ex-W.D. aluminium dories are available at bargain prices.

The 4-metre Commando, a French-made dory (more like a solid plastic inflatable) is an excellent, light and tough spear-fisherman's craft costing less than £500 at the time of writing.

Inflatables

The modern inflatable sportsboat is a far cry from the original rubber dinghy. It is a fast, light, manoeuvrable craft and can be carried on a trailer or car roof-rack. The air is contained in separate compartments, so in the event of a puncture the boat still floats.

Inflatables can be bought in kit form. If considering a second-hand boat, examine it most carefully for wear and patching.

As I have said, lightness and manoeuvrability are the inflatable's assets. They are very easy to get in and out of and will take a reasonable sea.

A disadvantage is exposure, more so than in a dory for you remain dry in only the calmest of seas and the ride is rather bumpy.

It goes without saying that extreme care must be taken with sharp objects. I once punctured one with the relatively blunt wheel on the manifold of a twin-bottle aqualung. In hot weather do not inflate too hard otherwise the seams may give as the air expands.

The inflatable can of course be deflated for transportation but most people keep them permanently inflated. If you do so, always clean sand and stones from the floor, specially where it meets the side compartments. If left it will wear the skin. If well looked after, useful life expectancy is about eight years.

A new 4-metre inflatable sells for around £800. I personally feel they are expensive for what they are in comparison to a fishing boat or dory.

Engines

To push a dory or inflatable with the ability to beat strong tides or the onset of bad weather, the engine needs to be at least 20 horsepower.

1. Competitors prepare for the 1960 British Championship at Looe. Three wear dry suits, the other, the now totally accepted wet suit

2. Masks and snorkels. *Left to right from top:* Pinocchio, Lince, Falco, Tubair, Minimax, Big G, Viso

3. Fins and a suitable knife. *Left to right:* Turnbull Giant, Cressi Professional, Beuchat Jetfin

4. 'Long John' trousers and two types of jacket

5. Floats with winder and fish-keep

6. Types of spear-head and examples of torches and rubbers

7. Compressed-air guns. *Left to right:* G.S.D. Dynamic, Mares Mirage, Cressi, Technisub Jaguar, Nemrod Clipper. A reel is also shown

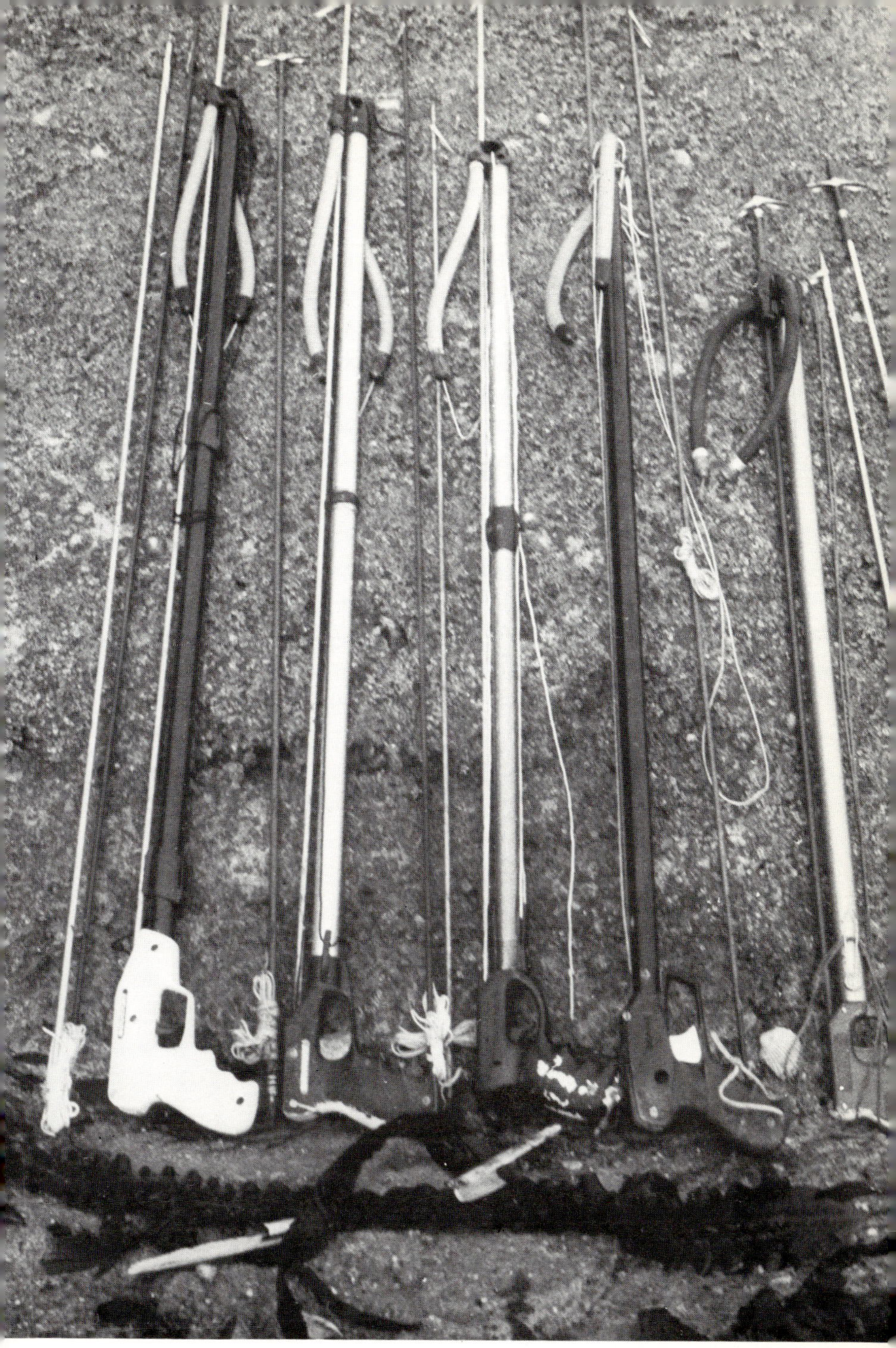

8. Rubber-powered guns. *Left to right:* Beuchat Marlin, Beuchat Caraibe, Sporasub, Marin Dyane, Champion Junior (original model)

9. A shingle beach offering the chance of all kinds of flat-fish. The far headland could provide pollack, bass, mullet and conger

10. A typical rocky beach. Mullet and bass are found inshore at high water, pollack off the headlands—and at low water, bass

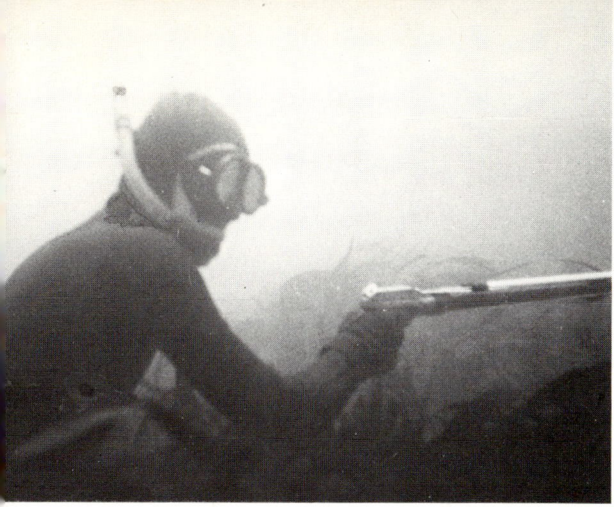

11. Keep still, finger on the trigger

12. Grip the speared fish firmly as you surface

13 Put the fish on the fish-keep before removing the spear

14. Kelp beds are often haunted by bass and mullet. The long fronds provide cover for the fishermen

If at all possible, buy a brand new engine with a good guarantee. A second-hand outboard is a gamble unless you know its history. The feeling whilst you drift in the tide as your mates curse at an obstinate engine is not very pleasant; outboards can be very temperamental. Have the engine regularly serviced and flush it through with freshwater after use.

When choosing an engine, special offers, long guarantees and so on have to be considered, but my own observations among divers and professional fishermen show the Mercury and Yamaha brands to be among the most popular. The four-stroke Honda is an excellent engine, but maximum size is, unfortunately, only 10 horsepower.

Safety

On any boat always carry an anchor and chain with rope equal to five times the depth of water, oars and rowlocks. Carry two spare plugs, tools, dry rags, red distress and smoke flares, all stored in a waterproof container, and a reserve of fuel. Fly the

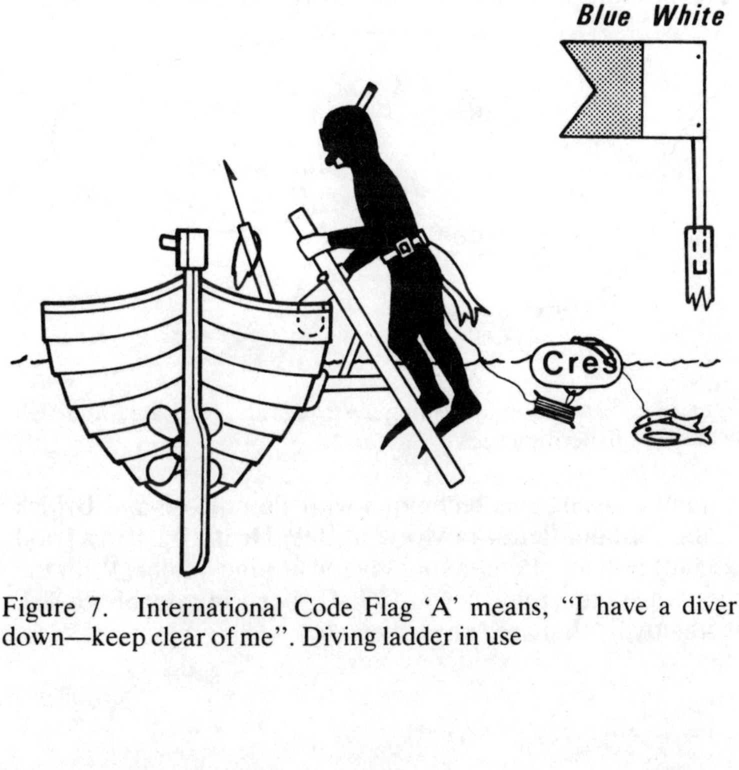

Figure 7. International Code Flag 'A' means, "I have a diver down—keep clear of me". Diving ladder in use

NATO Flag 4 when people are in the water—this flag means 'Divers are down, keep clear'.

Sometimes exhibitionists with more horsepower than sense will come too close, but you at least will be observing the correct procedure. A flag made from a rigid material such as marine plywood is preferable as in still conditions, a cloth flag is hardly visible unless you are on the move. On any boat where the gunwales are more than a metre from the water-line, a diving ladder (Fig. 7) makes life easier and prevents a lot of bruises. Fit stays to the ladder so that it stands off the side of the boat enabling you to enter and leave the water still wearing your fins. A sturdy, lockable locker is handy so that weight-belts, tools and such can be left on board.

A good example of the usefulness of a boat is when fishing in strong tide. Assuming there are three fishermen, one handles the boat while the other two enter the water up-tide, and fish. As they drift down the boat keeps just ahead and picks them up when they have passed over the best ground. The procedure is then repeated, someone else handling the boat. I

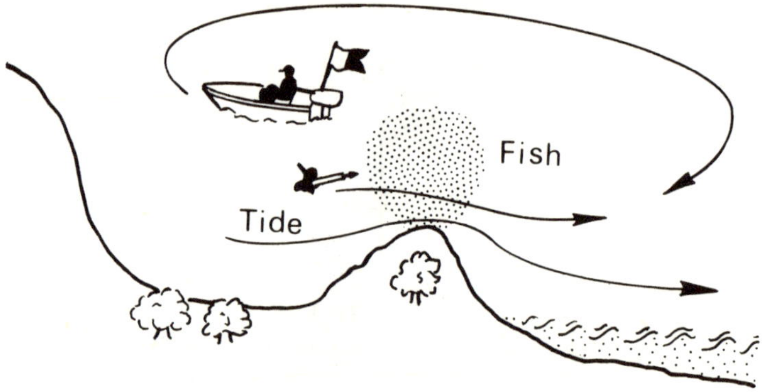

Figure 8. Technique for fishing in strong tide. Repeated until fish disperse or fisherman tires

remember using this technique with Tony Rose and British Team Captain, Pete Crawford, at Beer Head. We had a good catch of pollack, Pete taking several around 4 kilos. With the strength of the tide, it would have been impossible to fish productively that area any other way.

ABBREVIATED VERSION OF THE BEAUFORT WIND SCALE

Beaufort International Number (Force)	*Wind*	*Condition of Sea*
0	Calm	Mirror smooth.
1	Light Air	Small wavelets.
2	Light Breeze	Shorter more pronounced waves, crests breaking.
3	Gentle Breeze	
4	Moderate Breeze	Longer waves with 'white horses'.
5	Fresh Breeze	Long pronounced waves, foam crests everywhere.
6	Strong Breeze	Larger waves forming—more extensive foam crests.
7	Strong Wind	Sea heaping up, wind blowing foam in streaks.
8	Fresh Gale	Waves and crests increasing in height, foam blowing in dense streaks.
9	Strong Gale	
10	Whole Gale	High waves, long overhanging crests. Large patches of foam.
11	Storm	Very high waves hiding ship within sight in troughs. Sea covered with streaks of foam, air filled with spray.
12	Hurricane	

4

PHYSICAL CONSIDERATIONS AND DANGERS

In order to dive and catch fish beneath the sea, one does not have to be a veritable 'Tarzan', but a good general state of health is essential—if in doubt, consult your doctor. As a point of interest, the U.S.A. team which took third place in the 1959 and 1960 World Championships included Del Wren, a one-legged fisherman, who, at Malta, was timed at 1 minute 40 seconds for a 30-metre dive.

The would-be spearfisherman should have a sound heart and respiratory system. Any past history of middle-ear trouble or acute claustrophobia will bar participation in this sport. A steady temperament and ability to relax in the water is desirable.

During the early part of the year when bad weather and lack of fish make fishing a waste of time, road-running and sessions in a swimming pool will prepare you physically for the coming season. Some public swimming pools ban the use of fins and snorkel, except during club evenings, but ordinary swimming underwater and sustained surface swimming is still most beneficial. Unfortunately, heavy smoking and excessive alcohol are no great aids to breath-holding!

Continual diving and swimming—within one's capabilities—is fine, healthy exercise, but build up gradually. Do not stay in the water for six hours and try to dive to 10 metres on your first trip—there are plenty of fish to see in 3 metres of water. As you progress slowly, your body will become accustomed to the new conditions imposed upon it—your 'water fitness' will improve with each ensuing trip.

The Effects of Pressure on the Ears and Sinus Cavities

As one descends beneath the sea, the pressure on the body increases with depth. The body itself, having a high proportion of liquids, is virtually incompressible, but the lungs, middle-ear area and sinus cavities contain air at the normal atmospheric pressure of 1 kilo per square centimetre (14.7 pounds per square inch). As you swim down the pressure increases by 1 kilo per square centimetre every 10 metres; so at a depth of 10 metres (2 atmospheres) there is a pressure of 2 kilos on every square centimetre of your body—on an average-sized person this would be an overall pressure of 33 tonnes (34 tons). Whilst the rest of the body feels no discomfort, pain will be felt in the ears a metre or so beneath the surface. This pain is caused by the eardrum being forced in by the increasing pressure of water—a higher pressure than the 1 kilo per square centimetre that you took down with you from the surface. In order to prevent a ruptured eardrum, the ears must be 'cleared'. (The ears should in fact be cleared *before* pain is felt.)

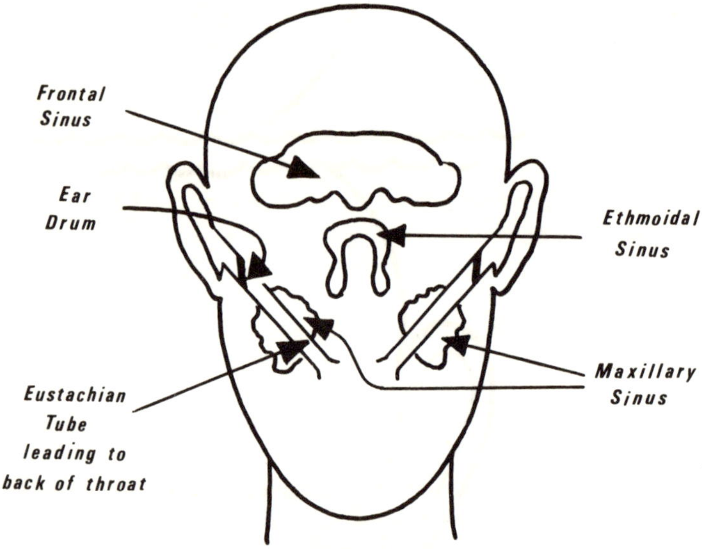

Figure 9. Sinuses and Eustachian tubes

As soon as you bend your waist and start to dive down, pinch your nose and gently blow; this will force air through the Eustachian tubes to the inside of the eardrum (the Eustachian tubes connect the back of the mouth with the inner ear) and

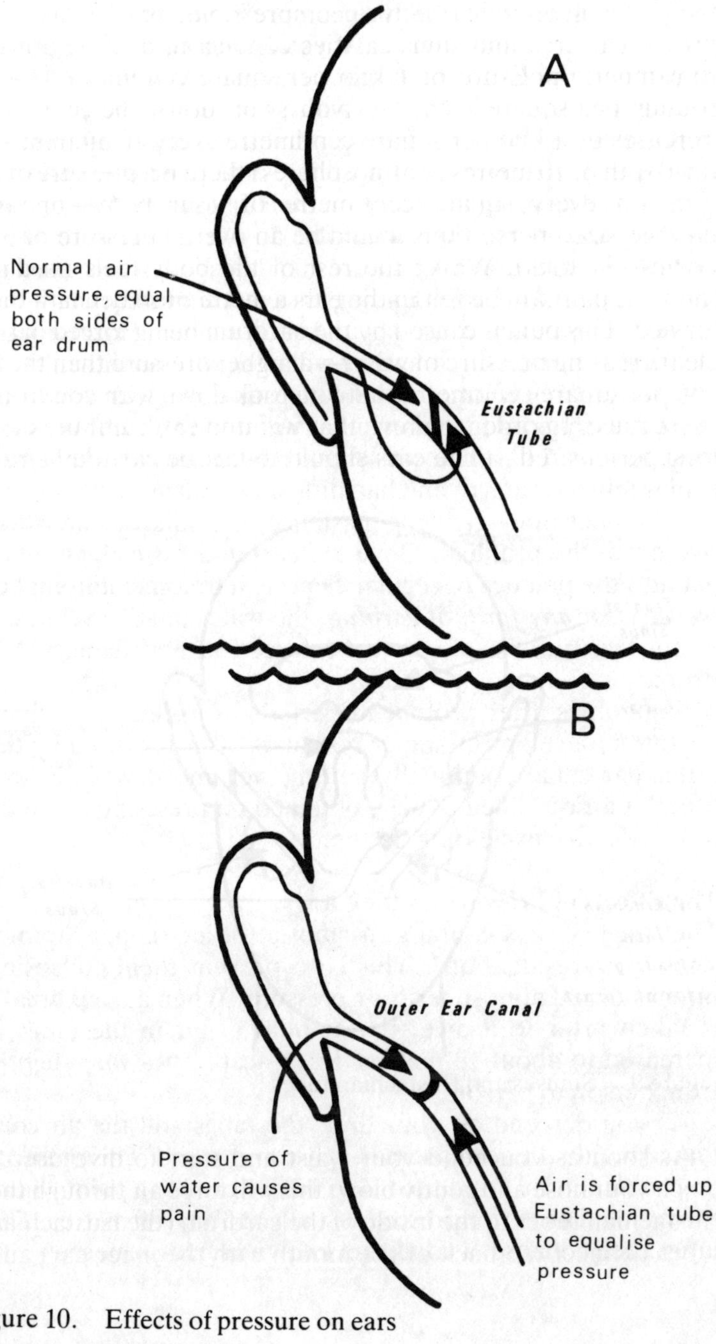

Figure 10. Effects of pressure on ears

the pain will disappear as the pressure is equalized. This also pressurizes the sinus cavities. If you have a cold or are prone to catarrh, the Eustachian tubes become blocked, as do the passages to the sinus cavities and it becomes difficult, if not impossible, to force air through them, so, never attempt to dive whilst suffering from a cold. Some people experience difficulty in clearing their ears on their first swims. If your ears do not clear at the first attempts, do not continue to swim down—an eardrum may rupture and damage can be caused to the delicate sinus tissues leading to severe complications—but leave the water and try again another time. Practise ear-clearing at home—in time they will click with no difficulty. If you suffer from a lot of nasal congestion see your doctor as there are drugs and inhalants that will disperse the mucus for long periods. I have known several newcomers who have had problems with catarrh and had difficulty in clearing their ears, but practice and *gentle* persistence in shallow water has overcome the problem. Once the ears and Eustachian tubes get into the practice of regular clearing it becomes automatic. *Never wear any form of earplug*, the water must have access to the eardrum; a plug will be forced in and damage the drum.

Sometimes after prolonged periods of fishing, an itching sensation develops in one or both ears. This is caused by the outer ear canal continually getting wet and drying. I have found a lotion called Synlar, obtained on prescription, to be most effective in clearing this up.

The Effects of Pressure on the Lungs

The lungs always contain an amount of air (about 3 pints) known as 'residual air'. This is to prevent them collapsing under normal atmospheric air pressure. When a deep breath is taken prior to a dive, the amount of air in the lungs is increased to about 12 pints (4 to 1)—capacities vary slightly from person to person.

As you descend on your dive, the lungs and the air contained within them are increasingly compressed. This presents no problem until the ratio of 4 to 1 is lowered to a point where the residual air is compressed, usually at about 30 metres. The lungs then collapse, a condition known as 'lung squeeze'.

Bearing these facts in mind, one may well ask how do men such as the Italian spearfisherman, Enzo Maiorca, and French-born Jacques Mayol accomplish their record breath-held dives. Maiorca has reached 87 metres, Mayol 92 metres—the present world record, established off Elba in October 1975. Also, how do the natives of the Tuamotu Islands, north-east of Tahiti descend to 40 metres as many as fifty times a day, staying submerged for up to 2 minutes a dive, collecting pearl shell?

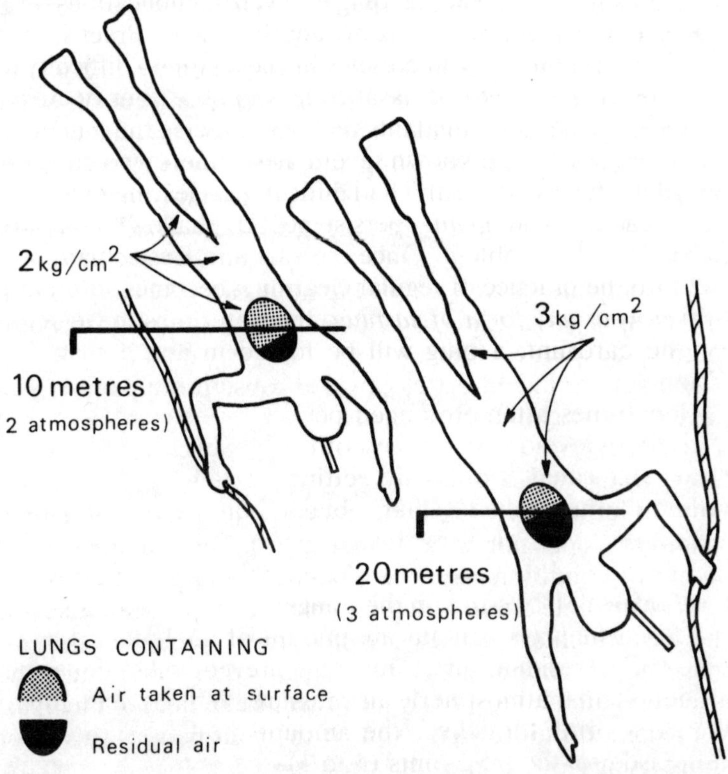

Figure 11. Effects of water pressure on the lungs and their air content.

In the cases of Mayol and Maiorca they have larger than average lung capacities, allowing for a greater degree of compression. Their attempts are carefully monitored by medical experts and they are escorted by experienced safety divers. Help and sophisticated equipment is provided by leading Italian equipment manufacturers. And, of course, they are simply prepared to accept a very great risk.

The Tuamotu islanders and all the peoples of the Pacific who dive and fish as part of their daily lives have been conditioned to this way of life and the stresses involved since childhood. Deep diving is almost as normal as walking, but even so, they have to keep within self-imposed limits or risk lung squeeze, eye haemorrhaging, headaches and general physical breakdown.

All the foregoing is in no way meant to encourage you to attempt 30-metre dives, but to show the effects of water pressure. The men capable of fishing at 30 metres and beyond have larger than normal lung capacities. This either occurs naturally or as a result of physical training and specific exercises, such as team training for international competitions.

The beginner is well advised to limit himself to depths of 8 or 9 metres. In fact, in British waters there is rarely any point in going deeper.

Pressure and cold water can also cause tooth pains if you have defective fillings in a cavity.

Other Dangers

Due to efficient insulation, cramp, the enemy of naked swimmers, does not often bother spearfishermen unless tired or out of condition. Although painful, cramp in itself is not dangerous unless you panic. Stomach cramp is rare and it is the legs which are usually affected, most frequently the calf muscles. If cramp takes you, keep calm—straighten the affected limb and force the toes back, catch hold of the tip of your fin and pull towards you. If the pain persists, head for shore using slow, shallow fin strokes.

Fish that bite or can inflict wounds with spines are dealt with in Chapter 6 with the exception of jellyfish and weevers, both potentially dangerous.

Jellyfish can give an unpleasant burning sensation if the tentacles come into contact with the bare skin. They are more abundant in hot weather—avoid them.

The weevers (greater and lesser) can inflict severe pain with their dorsal spines and deaths have been known in the case of elderly people or those with a weak heart. They lie buried in shallow, sandy bays with the spine erect and the chances of standing on one are rare. If you are unfortunate enough to be the 'one in a million' and stand on a weever, have the wound dressed with potassium permanganate. The greater weever grows to 40 cm.

As will be seen, our fish present us with few problems compared to our friends who fish in tropic waters.

Danger from Surface Craft

Nowadays the beaches around popular holiday resorts have flotillas of speed-boats and water-skiers, often dangerously close inshore 'playing to the gallery' of holidaymakers. If you find yourself in such a maelstrom of noise and quick thrills, keep your float close on a short line. If you hear a boat overhead, surface by coming up your float-line, looking up as you rise. Best of all, leave such places to our friends with a less contemplative nature than we have. Do not fish in the entrances to busy harbours or in recognized sea-lanes. Remember, sailing boats are silent, and do not innocently work on the assumption that all water users know (or even care) what your float represents.

The main danger to the beginner in British waters is over-enthusiasm and foolhardiness. So, progress slowly, learning as you go. Take a tip from the top spearfishermen and have a yearly check-up by your doctor, telling him that you intend to take up the sport. He can then make sure that the parts that matter are in good working order!

Artificial Respiration

Before we leave the gloomy but important subject of the dangers that can befall the spearfisherman, I think a few words on life-saving will not go amiss. The Royal Life-Saving Society, Desborough House, 14 Devonshire Street, Portland Place, London, W1N 2AT, publish an inexpensive, easy-to-understand book, *Life-Saving and Water Safety*. It covers expired air resuscitation (artificial respiration), methods of rescuing swimmers in distress, and the treatment for shock, cramp and the effects of cold and much more.

Many diving and swimming clubs run a life-saving course during the winter months, culminating in examinations for the R.L.S.S. Sub-Aqua Bronze Medallion.

There are many tragic incidents where a basic knowledge of expired air resuscitation could have saved a life and it only takes a few minutes to learn.

5

FISHING TECHNIQUES

Many parts of our coastline are suitable for spearfishing; the underwater visibility is the governing factor. The entire south-west of England, Dorset, Hampshire, Sussex and Yorkshire are all excellent areas. The Isle of Man and most of the Irish and Scottish coasts offer exciting possibilities. The waters of the Channel Islands are invariably clear and 'fishy'—Guernsey in particular. The local Press and angling journals give a good idea of the fish available throughout the country.

In all diving involving the use of mechanical breathing apparatus, the rule of always diving with a partner and keeping him within sight above and below the surface is sensible and also adds to the enjoyment. With spearfishing, diving together or, to be more precise, in close company, is not practicable, except in very clear water (20 metres plus visibility) or when tackling a large fish in a known location. Imagine the situation: you are on the bottom with a fish approaching when suddenly down fins your partner, promptly putting the fish to flight. Also, the possible outcome of two men in close proximity, firing at mid-water fish in bad visibility is obvious. Most of us go fishing with one or two friends, but once in the water, invariably go our separate ways, having different ideas on the most likely place to find fish. What I have said underlines the necessity of being a competent, confident swimmer in good physical condition.

Fishing Areas

When deciding upon an area of fish, think of the fish likely to be found there. If you have come to a wide, sandy beach (Plate 9) think in terms of flat-fish, such as plaice, sole, skate or ray. If you intend to swim from a boulder-strewn cove (Plate 10), think of round fish, such as bass, mullet or pollack.

High cliffs invariably mean deep water with caves and reefs. Where the coast is flat, it continues so underwater.

A flat, gently shelving beach is best for your first attempts. Always bear in mind the direction and strength of the wind on the days prior to your trip. It is most disappointing to arrive at a beach to find the sea has been thundering in all the week, making the water resemble soup; visibility of less than a metre makes fishing impossible, even with a short gun. Study weather forecasts and tide-tables (high water is generally clearer than low water) and how they will affect your chosen area before making a long journey. Remember that a sandy beach will 'stir up' and stay 'murky' more easily and for

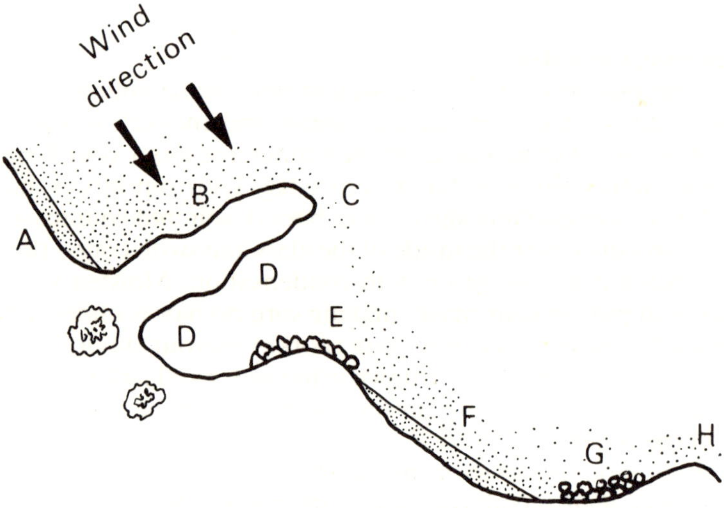

Figure 12. **Effect of wind on a stretch of coastline.** A. Sandy beach, nil to poor visibility. B. Cliffs, dirty water drifts along from 'A'. C. Tidal movement could mean slightly better visibility than 'B'. D. Good chance of clear water. E. Boulders at side of cove, clear water. F. Sandy beach, moderate visibility. G. Boulders, moderate visibility, but possible drift of dirty water from 'F'. H. Same condition as 'C'

longer, than a beach of rock and pebble. Often a headland will be 'murky' on the windward, but clear on the lee side, unless of course prolonged wind and successive tides have distributed dirty water along the whole coastline. If the wind has been light, only the first few metres may be dirty; clear water may be found by swimming a little way out—often the case on south-coast beaches. During May and June, particles of plankton and weed spores often hang suspended in the water, making visibility difficult until they metamorphose or are dispersed by spring tides.

Spring tides with their greater volume of water movement will make fishing difficult if not impossible at places such as headlands, estuaries and channels between off-shore rocks and the shore. If you are ever in doubt about tidal strength, always seek the advice of the local coastguard, fishermen, or a dive shop.

Entering the water

Having put on your suit and weight-belt, make your way to the water's edge, carrying gun, mask and snorkel, fins and float. Unwind some line from the winder and moor your float a few metres out from the water's edge. Dip your fins in the water (this helps them slip on over boots); spit into your mask and rub saliva over the inside of the glass and swill it out—this will prevent it misting up with condensation. Moisten your face and put on your mask, making sure no hair is under the edges to cause leaks; put your snorkel in your mouth and wade out to your float. Lie down in the water and pick up your float-weight. Swim out, gun in one hand, towing your float with the other.

When you are away from the shore and any swimmers—*and only then*—load your gun with the safety-catch on. If using a rubber gun, make sure the spear is locked in the trigger housing and whilst standing or treading water, place the butt against your stomach, just above your weight-belt. Gripping the rubbers just in front of the wishbone, pull them back keeping your hands together; letting them move apart as you pull can result in a broken wishbone. Hook the wishbone into one of the notches on the spear. If you find it hard to pull straight back to the full-power notch, hook into the first notch, rest and then pull back to the second. Arrange the line freely along the gun, hooking it under the clip in front of the butt.

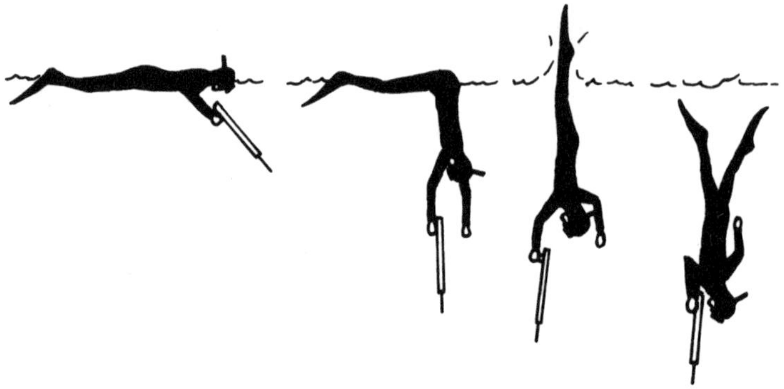

Figure 13. Diving technique for (A) Round fish (B) Flat-fish

If using a compressed-air gun; tread water, place the back of the hand-grip on your knee—keeping the muzzle out of line with your face. Put the end of the spear into the muzzle and push the spear down until it clicks—do not forget your loader if the gun has not got a power regulator. Arrange the line along the barrel and secure with the rubber clip or hook.

Turn over onto your face and swim on, gun in front—elbow slightly bent, float trailing about 5 metres behind. In British waters it is often difficult, from the surface, to discern the type of bottom you are swimming over in only a few metres depth. Drop your float-weight, paying off line from the winder; when the weight is on the bottom, pay off a few more metres and secure the line. Execute the normal dive, bending at the waist and throwing up the legs, pick up your float and weight and surface. Swim on, diving every so often.

Fishing for Round Fish

If the bottom is rocky with weeds, lie prone, holding on with the hand that is holding the float-weight—if the bottom looks 'fishy' release the float-weight. Lie still, gun in front, finger on the trigger, safety-catch off, (Plate 11). Move your head slowly from side to side; if you see a fish freeze! When the fish appears to be within 2 metres—preferably less—fire! Note I say appears. Objects seen underwater appear a third larger and closer due to the lights rays bending as they enter the water. This phenomenon, called refraction, causes no real

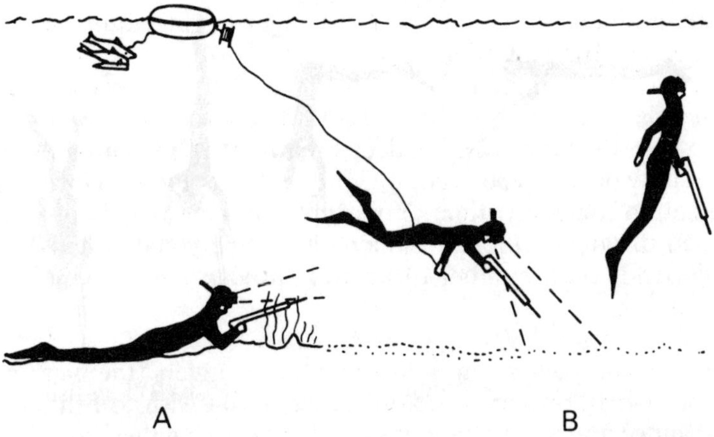

problem and one soon adapts to it, but at this early stage try to avoid long shots that may result in merely wounding.

If a fish is hit, get hold of it quickly (Plate 12). Gripping the fish firmly, kill it and thread it on your float or belt fish-keep whilst it is still on the spear (Plate 13), then remove the spear. A floating type of gun can be released while you handle the fish. A non-floating gun can be held between the knees, or if the water is shallow, allowed to fall to the bottom. Never pull a fish hard towards you by the spear-line unless sure it is well on the spear. A lightly hit fish can break off if the line is tugged vigorously.

This is the basic approach for all round fish (bass, mullet, etc.). I shall deal with variations for different fish in Chapter 6. Do not worry about precise aiming in the accepted sense—an underwater gun is fired more by instinct, like a cowboy's revolver—and not aimed in the manner of a rifle.

Fishing for Flat- and Bottom Fish

If you dive and find a bottom of sand or shingle, swim along a few metres off the bottom, looking in all directions for a sign of a 'flat'. Successful flat-fishing requires a lot of dives, methodically searching areas of sand and shingle—do not forget to survey patches of sand amongst rocks and bordering reefs. A good tip for fishing in deep water is to paint or bind the handle of your gun with white paint or P.V.C. tape, making it more easily visible from the surface if it has to be abandoned. A large angler or conger might require several dives to bring it to the surface.

Whilst swimming on the surface, breathe normally and regularly through your snorkel. When you decide to dive, exhale and take in a good deep breath then glide smoothly and quietly down. A 30-second, 5-metre dive is good—a lot can be seen in that short time. Your 'bottom times' will improve as you progress although the length of time you can stay down depends on a number of factors—fitness, lung capacity and training.

If, during your swim, you come upon anglers (the men, not the fish!) between you and the area you wish to fish, swim inshore and under their lines, acknowledging them as you do so. Do not hang around, diving in their immediate vicinity, this only leads to abuse, stone-throwing and cases have been known where irritated anglers have tried to hook divers with mackerel feathers. The same applies with professional fishermen. Diving in the vicinity of moored nets or pots in full view of their owners is asking for trouble and sooner or later you will get it. Conversely, if you are fishing a certain spot and anglers appear, carry on fishing; it is a matter of who is there first. In some cases, the more serious and proficient angler is only too keen to give and take advice.

An hour or so will be enough for your first attempt; do not overdo things—staying down so long that the desire to breathe becomes uncomfortable, or diving too deep. Get into the water as often as you can, letting your body gradually adapt to the strains being imposed upon it. Unload your gun by firing or releasing the rubbers whilst still in the water and away from any swimmers.

Hyperventilation

There is a practice used by many spearfishermen—especially in competition—to increase their bottom time on deep dives. This widely condemned method, known as hyperventilation, is effective but can be highly dangerous. As you are bound to come across it sooner or later, I feel its full implications should be understood at the outset.

The urge to breathe is triggered by the building up of

carbon dioxide (CO_2) and not by lack of oxygen as may be thought. Normally the CO_2 is breathed away, but when the breath is held it builds up until it reaches a point where you feel the need to breathe. On a normal breath-held dive you should then surface. When hyperventilating prior to a dive, six or more deep breaths are taken, flushing out the normal residue of CO_2 contained in the lungs. As there is now much less CO_2 in the lungs, the build-up and subsequent warning is much slower in coming. The fisherman stays below, not feeling the urge to breathe, but oxygen is still being extracted from the air in his lungs; experience tells him when to surface. But if he stays submerged too long (three minutes or more) the oxygen becomes exhausted and the brain, having a high oxygen requirement, ceases to function—he blacks out and drowns as a result of anoxia (oxygen starvation). There is a further complication. At depths exceeding 10 metres the pressure of water on the chest compresses the lungs (see Chapter 4) and increases the air pressure. This is important because the oxygen in the lungs is now under a greater pressure. At this higher pressure the lungs are able to absorb a higher percentage of oxygen than normal. The fisherman is in fact able to stay down longer at depth than in shallow water, but as he starts to ascend the partial pressure of the oxygen drastically decreases (absorption of oxygen is proportional to pressure changes), the fisherman can therefore simply run out of oxygen on his way to the surface and suffer a blackout.

It is generally agreed that *minimal* hyperventilation—i.e. holding the third breath—is safe. For all normal purposes one good breath is more than adequate.

As you progress, increasing your bottom times and the duration of your swims, you will notice on surfacing from a dive that your heart rate increases and you have to rest before diving again. This period between dives is known as the 'recovery time'. To shorten your recovery time, blow the water out of your snorkel as soon as you surface, take a few breaths, then hold your breath for 10 seconds or so. When the breath is held and the supply of oxygen is cut off, the heart pumps slowly to conserve the amount of oxygen in the lungs;

so this act of holding your breath decreases your heart rate back to near normal and enables you to dive again without too much delay. In competition fishing, the shorter your recovery time the longer you spend under water over the period of the competition—increasing your chances of catching fish.

As I have stressed before, progress slowly and steadily and study weather, tides and terrain. Always remember one thing—the man in the right place, at the right time, catches fish. But the fittest, best-equipped man in the world is useless without a sound understanding of the habits of his quarry.

6

SPECIES—THEIR HABITS AND CAPTURE

I shall deal only with the fish worthy of the spearfisherman's attention for their sporting and edible qualities. There is no point in discussing foreign species that occasionally stray to our shores—fish that cannot be seriously hunted, or deep water fish such as ling and hake that the fisherman may never see underwater in a lifetime. The British Records (*see* Appendix II) list a number of fish of which I make no mention; for the same reasons. They are the once in a lifetime catch, recorded over nearly thirty years of spearfishing.

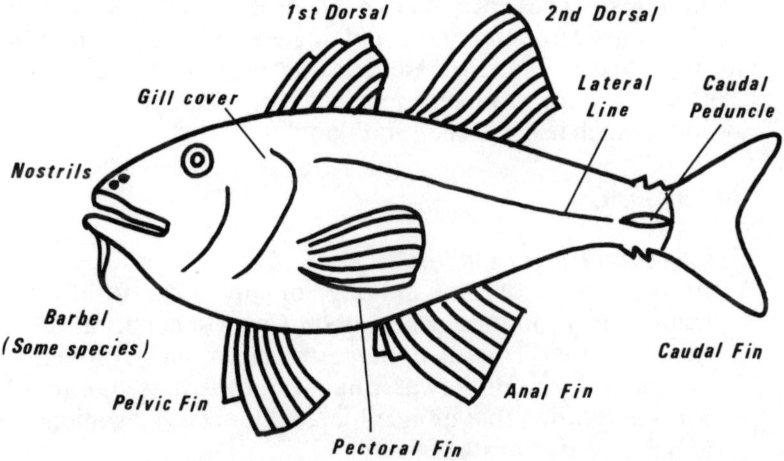

Figure 14. Features of a typical fish

Fish are divided into classes, orders, and families within their order.

Class SELACHII (Cartilaginous skeleton)

Order Pluerotremata:	shark, dogfish, monkfish.
Order Hypotremata:	ray, skate.

Class PISCES (Bony skeleton)

Order Apodes:	conger.
Order Synentognathi:	garfish.
Order Anacanthini:	cod, pollack, pouting.
Order Zeomorphi:	John Dory.
Order Percomorphi:	bass, red mullet, bream, wrasse, mackerel, grey mullet.
Order Scleroparei:	gurnard.
Order Heterosomata:	turbot, brill, plaice, dab, flounder, sole, lemon sole.
Order Pediculati:	angler.

For practical purposes the British spearfishermen divide their fish into two categories:

Round Fish. As the name implies, these are round-bodied fish that swim freely in mid-water or just off the sea bed. Some are resident British fish, others migratory.

Bottom Fish. These are fish that live on or near the bottom. It could be argued that conger and dogfish are 'round fish', but as they live and are speared on the bottom we call them bottom fish. In competitions they are awarded the same points as such fish as plaice and skate.

Round Fish

BASS (*Dicentrarchus labrax*).

> 'Is there any form of hunting, or any other form of fishing, on a continent where nature has lost her primeval savagery that can give modern man such profound emotions as the underwater hunt after the bass? Or any form of hunting that obliges him to adopt such ingenious and dangerous stratagems.'
>
> *The Underwater Naturalist*, Pierre De Latil, Jarrolds, 1954.

Bass is the most sought after British sporting sea fish and is found all around the coast, but mainly in the south. It has a magnificent appearance with a metallic blue back, silver sides and white belly. There are two dorsal fins, the first having

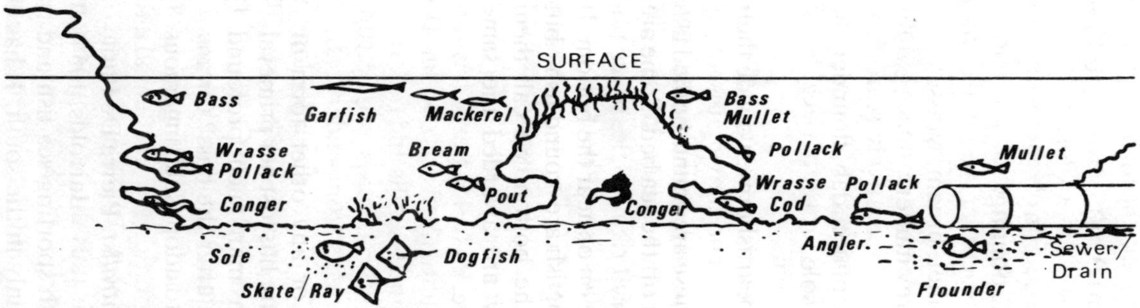

Figure 15. Typical section of sea bed and fish locations

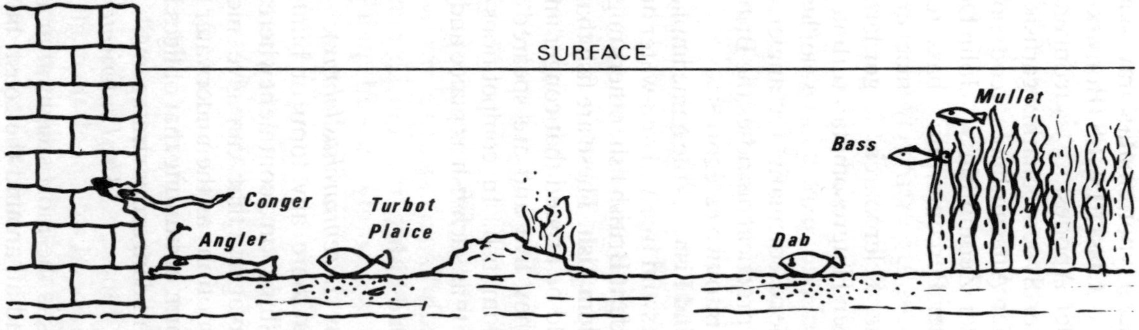

Figure 16. Wall or breakwater inhabitants. Watch out for boat traffic

eight or nine spines. The gill covers have razor-sharp edges, so this fish must be handled with care.

Bass frequent off-shore reefs and rocky headlands, coming inshore to spawn in May and June. A slow-growing fish, it takes up to twenty years for a bass to reach 4 kilos.

As far as we are concerned, bass are rarely met with until the beginning of June and then through until the end of November, with September and October being the best months.

Bass are extremely wary and movement or noise will put them to flight. The larger fish are comparatively scarce and totally unpredictable in their movements. The newcomer should not expect large catches of bass—twenty sizeable fish in a season is good for an experienced man.

As said before, bass favour rocky headlands and off-shore reefs, hunting these areas at low tide and moving inshore as the tide rises. When you have swum out to a likely area, dive quietly down to the top of the rocks and settle in the kelp, trying if possible to position yourself at right-angles to the tide and facing downstream (bass invariably swim head-on to the tide so that food is brought to them). It is often not necessary to dive more than 4 metres and if you are lucky bass will appear; the larger fish of 2½ kilos or more, singly, or in pairs, the smaller fish in shoals of anything up to 15. Large bass are mostly 'loners'. Keep perfectly still until the fish are within 1½ metres range, then quickly aim behind the gills and fire. If the fish is securely speared, pull it gently towards you, getting your thumb and index finger in its gills from underneath as soon as possible; never let any fish 'flap' on a spear for longer than you can possibly help as they may rip off and be lost. Kill it and thread it on your fish-keep, as described in Chapter 2. If your shot was unsuccessful, surface, reload and continue diving, moving forward; there may be other bass in the area. When you see a bass, resist the temptation to look behind it to see if there is a bigger one—the chances are the movement of your head will spook them all, their tails thudding audibly in the water as they disperse in all directions. Always make use of any available cover—rocks, weed and debris. Hold your gun out in front of you to increase its range (few guns have any penetrative power beyond 3 metres). Bass like areas where

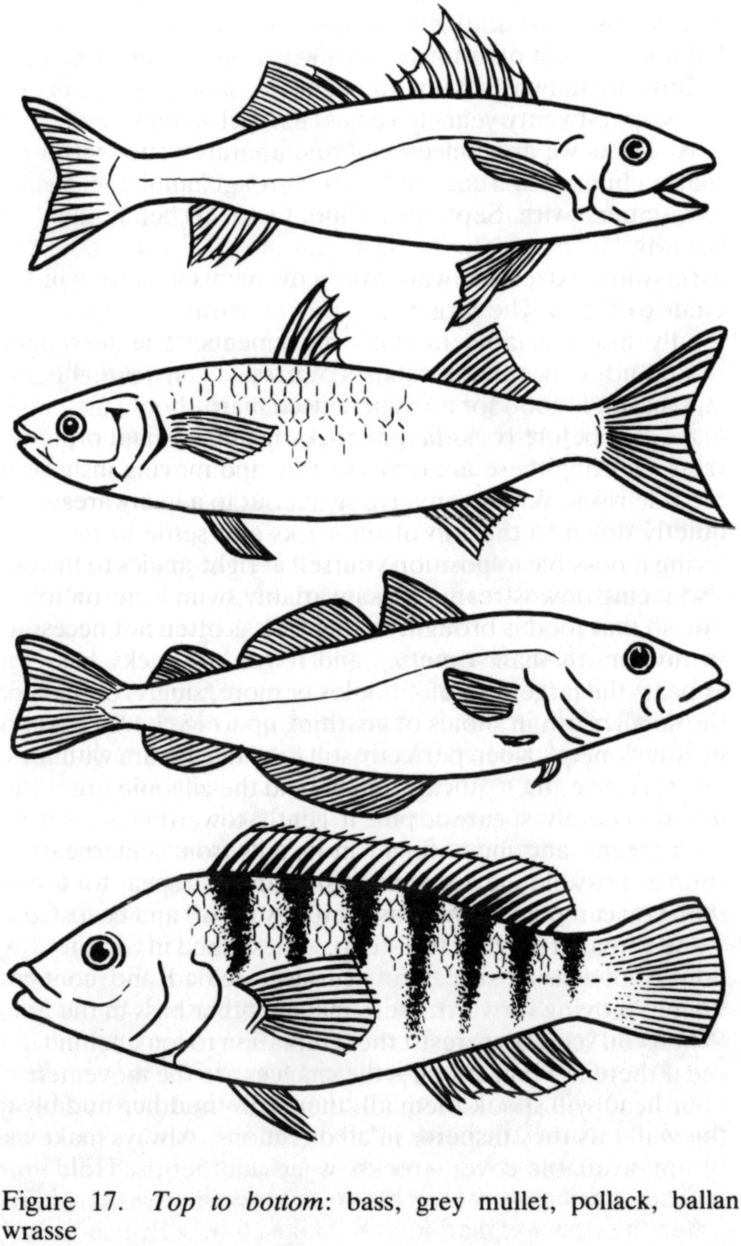

Figure 17. *Top to bottom*: bass, grey mullet, pollack, ballan wrasse

the tidal movement is strong, but do not venture into tide that you cannot swim against; fish the edges of a tidal 'run'. The beginner should avoid swimming with a strong outgoing tide.

Bass sometimes frequent estuaries and the vicinity of harbours. If an area has plenty of small fish, crabs and sand-eels, there is a good chance of finding bass. Often when the sea has been rough they will come inshore looking for worms and shellfish that have been churned up. At these times the sea will be too murky for fishing, but when it has cleared a little, then is the time to go. When the 'vis' is poor there is less chance of the fish seeing you.

In some areas bass and mullet can be found under ledges; the plates of wrecks or holes in the rock. Portland, Bognor Rocks and the area around Poole Harbour are good examples. Quietly look under such cover, finger on the trigger, ready to fire as soon as you see a fish. There is a hole in a rock in the Sussex area where 4–5 kilo bass are regularly taken by those who know its exact position.

Bass are very edible. Before leaving the subject of bass I think mention should be made of what must be the most enviable capture in the history of British spearfishing and of two other catches of note.

In 1970, Colin House of the Weymouth Club was fishing in Portland Harbour. With bass in mind, he headed for a wreck he knew, where he had taken a 4½ kilo bass the previous day. On reaching the outskirts of the wreck, he took a 1¼ kilo mullet and then moved on to the main structure. After preliminary dives he found a barge, entered a hole and swam two metres inside it. He was about to move further in when he saw a large tail. The bass moved further into the wreck. Colin slipped out through the side of the barge and swam along hoping to cut the fish off. He waited by a hole at the other end but the bass did not appear. Looking in through the hole he saw the largest bass he had ever seen. As he raised his gun the fish moved off; Colin immediately fired and headed, out of breath, for the surface. Keeping his line taut he then swam down in through the hole. There in the now muddy water was the bass. Colin put his hands in its gills and surfaced. He soon realized this fish was larger than his previous best of 7 kilos. Later the bass weighed in at 8.7 kilos, a new British record.

The world record for bass stands at 13.38 kilos for a fish taken by the ex-world team and French champion, Hughes Dessault from Marseille.

At the 1979 Sussex National competition held in September at Saltdean, Brian Carlson had a memorable catch. He took eight bass with a total weight of 35 kilos as well as five mullet and a conger. Burdened by this catch, Brian was late arriving at the finish of the competition and put on half-points but still took fourth place. But Brian is the first to admit that his catch must take second place to the eight bass (best fish 5 kilos) taken by Jonce Weedon to win the 1969 Southsea B.S-A.C. National at Selsey Bill. Jonce utilized a discarded tin bath to get his fish from the beach to the scales. Perhaps clubs organizing competitions along the Sussex coast could arrange for a supply of similar baths (suitably reinforced and drilled for drainage) to be left at various vantage points!

MULLET (*Chelon labrosus*). Only the thick-lipped grey mullet will really concern us. Other species such as the thin-lipped and golden mullets are less frequently met with and in any case would be fished for in the same manner as the thick-lipped.

A streamlined fish, the mullet has a leaden, grey-blue back with dark horizontal stripes on the flanks, the belly is white. The first dorsal fin has four spines.

Mullet migrate in large shoals into British coastal waters in the summer months, entering harbours, estuaries and swimming up freshwater rivers. Muliet and bass often swim together, but mullet are more often seen—predominantly in the southern part of the British Isles—and are really the mainstay of the British fisherman.

Mullet are found off most beaches in the summer months. They are particularly fond of sewer outfalls (if you can stand it!) and where fresh water enters the sea. The beds of 'string weed' (*Chorda filum*) are favourite haunts of mullet and bass.

The fishing technique is similar to bass. Mullet move in over rocks and weed at high water, looking for algae, bits of weed and decomposing matter. Dive quietly, settle among whatever cover is available and look up. When mullet appear—generally in twos or threes—wait until you can get a shot high on the body, as a mullet shot in the soft belly will likely as not tear itself off the spear. If you 'gut shoot' a mullet, drop your gun and grab the fish as quickly as firmly as possible, just behind the head.

A mullet of 2 kilos is a good fish. The flesh has a similar taste to bass, but is not as good.

POLLACK (*Pollachius pollachius*). This fish has a dark green back, yellow-brown sides and a grey belly. The lower jaw juts out farther than the upper and the lateral line curves over the pectoral fin. These last two features distinguish it from its near relative the coalfish. Found all around Britain, pollack and the rarer coalfish share the same ground, habits and fishing technique. Pollack can be found in large shoals from May to November, sometimes later. The shoal fish tend not to exceed 1½ kilos; larger fish being solitary or in pairs.

Deep gullies and dark caves and ledges on reefs are favoured by pollack—a common but roaming fish. As you glide down the side of a reef, hang on to a rock or kelp stalk and peer under overhangs and into shadowy recesses—always avoid unnecessary movement. If a pollack is there, hovering, fire. Aim for the top of the gills if possible. When shot, get your fingers in the gills the same as with bass (the same applies to any large fish—the piece of bone connecting the bottom of the jaw with the forward end of the stomach affords a good handhold). As you settle on the top of a reef, small shoal pollack will appear; wait as long as you can because often a bigger fish will follow them up from deeper water.

Small shoaling pollack of half a kilo are often found aimlessly drifting over a patch of sand, among kelp-strewn rocks and are easy prey. Fish of 2 kilos or more are a different matter, sometimes requiring dives of 10 metres to find them.

The flesh of the pollack is plain, but quite edible.

WRASSE Ballan (*Labrus bergylta*). The largest member of the wrasse family, the ballan is the only one worth shooting. The mouth is small with distinct teeth; the body coloured in dashes of red, brown and green. The fins are red with white spots. Wrasse are found all around the British Isles, mainly off the west coasts. One and a half kilo fish are common.

A territorial fish, wrasse are found on all types of bottom and at all depths. They like to hide in the stalks of kelp, holes and ledges. Often as you lie quietly on the bottom a wrasse will drift up, flit away, drift back and flit away again.

Wrasse are fairly easy fish to shoot, so please do not use them for target practice or for the sake of shooting something. The flesh is rather soft and plain, but not altogether disagreeable. In the Channel Islands they are baked and in France form an essential part of the famous *bouillabaisse*.

COD (*Gadus morhua*). Most people are familiar with the cod, if only in fish-finger form. They have a large head with the mottled green-red body tapering to a small tail.

Because cod generally only come inshore in the winter months—hunting behind the surf—they are rarely taken by spearfishermen. The notable exceptions are the Scarborough area in Yorkshire (during the 1970 Yorkshire competition Wally Pack from Sussex shot cod of 6 and 7 kilos), and Sussex, where members of the Sussex Spearfishing Club have also taken fine hauls of big cod from wrecks and ledges along their coast. The fish 'hole-up' and a torch can be very useful. I took my only cod, a fish of 5½ kilos, at Hallsands, Devon in thick January drizzle. Most of the cod speared, seem to be in the 3–6 kilo range.

MACKEREL (*Scomber scombrus*). Everyone is familiar with the mackerel, with its distinctive tuna-like appearance. Most often met with near the surface chasing sand-eels, the mackerel is a satisfying bonus fish, its speed calling for a quick shot. In Channel Island competitions extra points are awarded for mackerel.

GARFISH (*Belone Belone*). You will often see 'gars' in the vicinity of mackerel. They have a silver-blue eel-like body, up to 75 cm long, with a needle snout. The garfish is a difficult target as it circles you, just under the surface. A thin spear is a help in securing the 3 cm deep body. Both garfish and mackerel are usually seen on hot, still, summer days. The flesh of the garfish is good to eat and is reputed to have medicinal qualities.

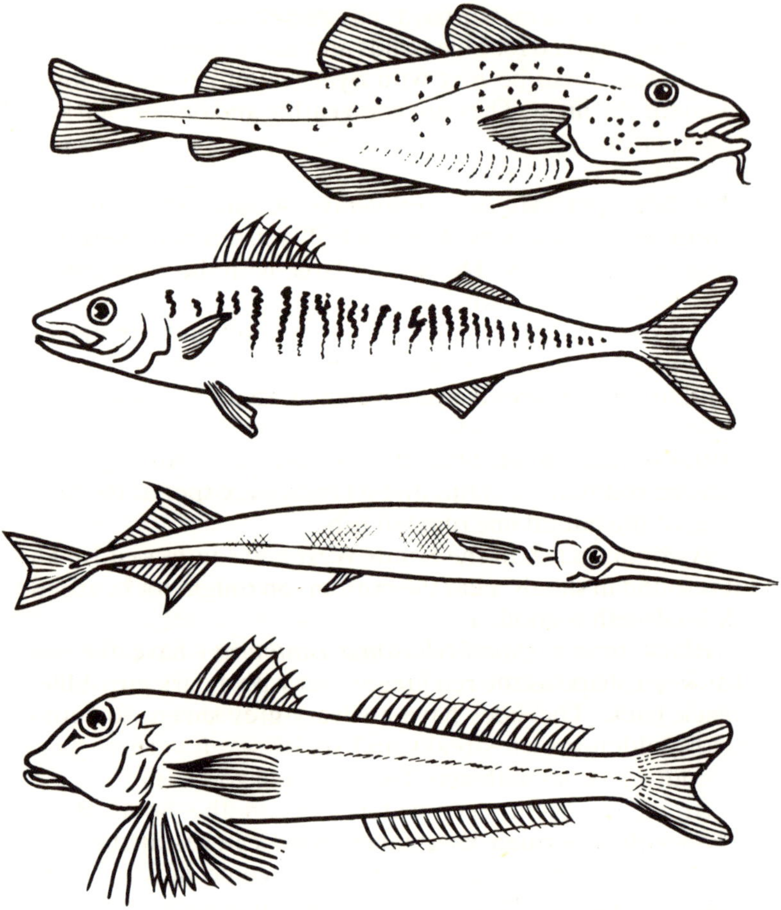

Figure 18. *Top to bottom*: cod, mackerel, garfish, gurnard

GURNARDS. There are three gurnards of interest to us. The grey gurnard (*Eutrigla gurnardus*); red gurnard (*Aspitrigla cuculus*); tub gurnard (*Trigla lucerna*).

The gurnards have a large head, with the body tapering back from armoured, spined gill plates. The lower three rays of the pectoral fins are feeling organs with which the fish searches the bottom for food. The names describe the colouring of the grey and red gurnards; the tub, sometimes called the saphirine gurnard, has deep blue pectoral fins with an orange-red edge, blue bands and green spots.

Gurnards will be met with over smooth, sandy bottoms. Aim for the head. They are good eating and one of .900 kilo is a good fish.

RED MULLET (*Mullus surmuletus*). A rare fish, confined to south and west coasts. It has a brilliant red body with three longitudinal stripes. The head is large with the body tapering to a deeply forked tail.

The red mullet is highly prized as food and commands a high price. You may, if lucky, come across a small shoal over sand or mud. The maximum weight is about 1.50 kilos.

BREAM Red bream (*Pagellus bogaraveo*). This fish has an orange-red body and fins and a large black spot at the beginning of the lateral line of adult fish.

A common fish in the South-West and south-west Ireland, it is found in shoals, near the bottom, on rough, rocky ground. A 1-kilo fish is good.

Black bream (*Spondyliosoma cantharus*) have the same thick-set shape as the red bream, but with a dark grey-blue or black back. The sides have a silvery-grey sheen, sometimes with golden-brown streaks and six or seven vertical bands. Colouring varies with age. Two kilos is a good fish.

Bream frequent deep-water reefs in the South-West—Plymouth fishermen have taken good catches at the Eddystone—but on the Sussex coast they come into water of a couple of metres. Here they are sometimes seen while fishing for bass and mullet. A thick, good eating fish, the smaller specimens are not particularly wary.

POUTING (*Trisopterus luscus*). Pouting have a deep, bronze body with dark vertical bands, a large eye and a barbel on the chin. There is a spot at the base of the pectoral fin. Pout live in caves and under ledges; the larger specimens in water of 10 metres or more.

A torch and short gun are useful when searching holes for pout. They will be seen hovering in the shadows. They have soft flesh, so aim high and grab the fish as soon as you can.

Figure 19. *Top to bottom*: red mullet, bream, pouting, conger

Although of a general distribution, we see most of our pout at Sussex. Large shoals move over the crumbly, clay rocks. They are, however, mainly small, often mingling with bream of the same size. It is a magical experience to lie quietly on the bottom at Hove, with large shoals of 12 cm pout in all directions—but not one worth shooting! Pout are quite good eating but gut as soon as possible. They grow to 2½ kilos, but a 1-kilo fish is good.

JOHN DORY (*Zeus Faber*). An odd-shaped fish, rather like a flat-fish swimming on its side. Olive-brown colouring with a black spot inside a yellow ring just behind the pectoral fins (according to legend, the spot is St Peter's thumbprint). Found over sand and sandy patches amongst rocks, although not a rare fish few are taken by spearfishermen, but strangely enough and to my great satisfaction, a John Dory was the third or fourth fish I shot when I first took up the sport!

Bottom Fish (Flat-fish)

In Chapter 5 I described the dive-and-search technique for flat-fish. Once a 'flat' is seen, fire immediately, 4 or 5 cm behind the eyes. If you do not expect to see round fish on your trip, a hand-spear is sufficient for flats.

Unlike round fish, flat-fish are resident for most of the year. Although not strictly flat-fish, I include conger and dogfish under this heading since they are met with on the sea bottom and with the same searching dives. A general rule to remember when looking for flats: the type of ground over which you are swimming will dictate the type of fish to be found.

PLAICE (*Pleuronectes platessa*). The best known flat and one of Britain's most popular food fish. They have an oval, dark green-brown body with distinctive orange spots. They have a preference for 'bitty' as opposed to soft sand or mud and are found all around Britain.

Plaice can be fished for all the year round and fill the gap left by the migratory round fish. As with all flats, aim behind the eyes to avoid spoiling the flesh. Push your fish-keep through

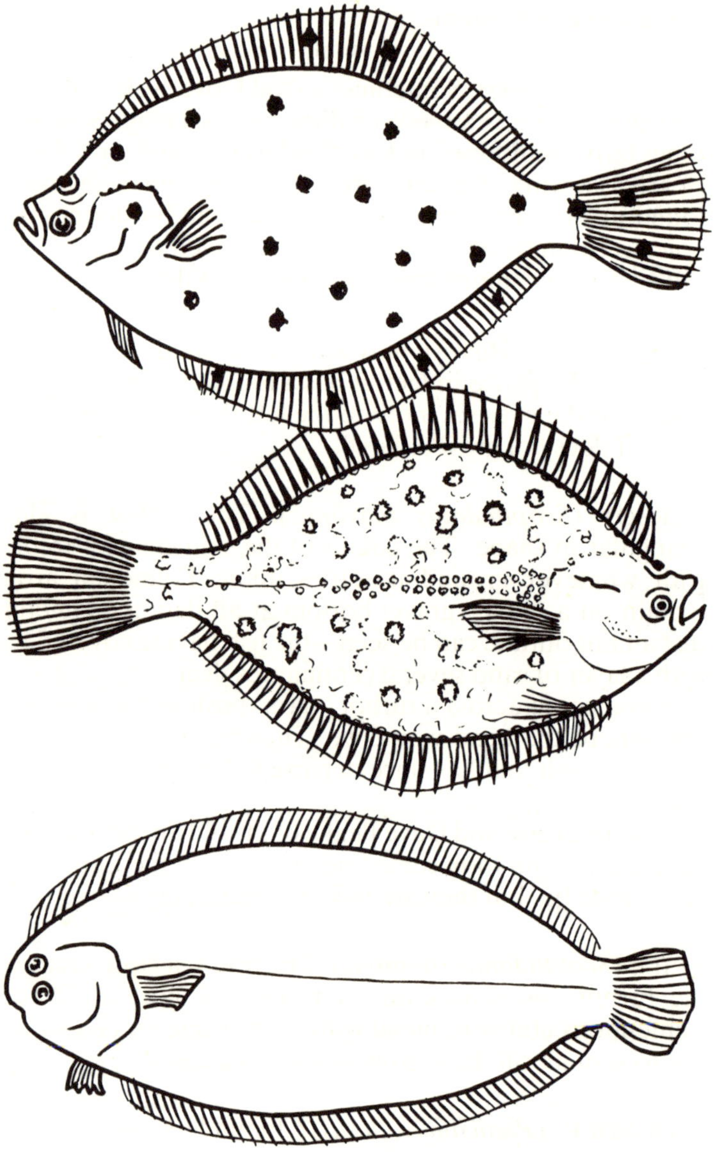

Figure 20. *Top to bottom*: plaice, flounder, common sole

the thick part of the head. A good fish is 1½ to 2 kilos—3 kilos being about maximum.

SOLE (*Solea solea*). Sometimes called Dover sole. I think the best description is a piece of dirty, oval sacking. Sole sometimes bury themselves under a thin layer of sand, only the eyes clearly showing. Occasionally, three or four sole may be found in close proximity on a strip of sand bordering rocks. Sole are sometimes found among, and even on top of, small rocks. The maximum weight is about 2½ kilos.

LEMON SOLE (*Microstomus kitt*). Unrelated to the sole—a cousin of the plaice in fact, it has a rounder, lemon-coloured body and the eyes set more to the left than those of the sole. Also, it does not grow as large.

TURBOT (*Scopthalmus maximus*). The turbot is almost triangular in shape. The colour of the skin changes to blend with whatever ground it settles upon. Found all around Britain on a 'bitty', gravel bottom at all depths. Sometimes just a faint outline can be seen—the fish having covered itself with a layer of sand several centimetres deep.

If you come across a turbot 'mark' push or fire your spear into where the head would be. Then again, it could be the mark of a fish that has since departed. Turbot weigh up to 24 kilos.

Arnold Cruise and Dave Peake of the old Spearfishing Club of Great Britain took some fine turbot from the Looe area in years gone by, but they are now becoming very scarce.

BRILL (*Scopthalmus rhombus*). The brill is a close relative of the turbot and shares the same kind of ground. It has a tremendous ability to blend with the bottom—it takes a good eye to spot a brill. Brill grow to about 4 kilos.

FLOUNDER (*Platichthys flesus*). Flounders are similar in appearance to the plaice, but have fewer, paler orange spots. They have spines on lateral line, anal and dorsal fins. Flounders are found mainly on soft sand or mud, particularly

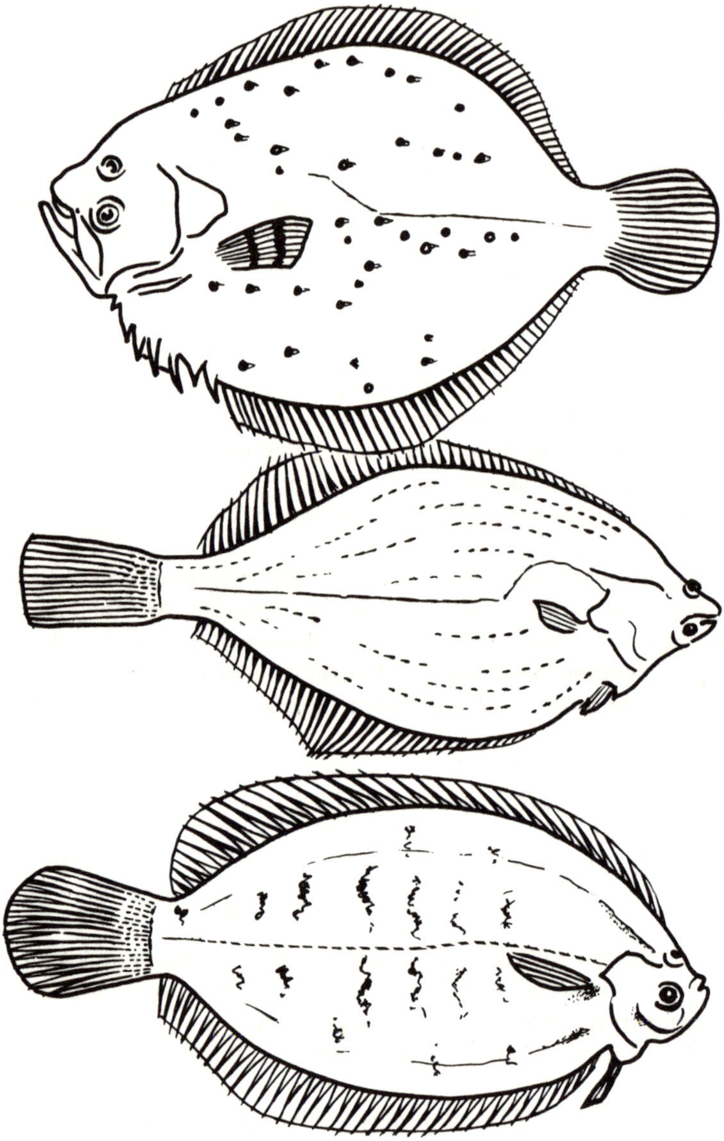

Figure 21. *Top to bottom*: turbot, dab, lemon sole

in estuaries and rivers of low salinity and in depressions where dead weed has accumulated. They grow to 2½ kilos.

The flesh of the flounder tends to be watery unless kept a day before eating.

DAB (*Limanda limanda*). Dabs are light brown with darker spots and sometimes a few orange ones. They are found in shallow, sandy bays all around Britain. Dabs are sometimes confused with other flats; if in doubt, run your finger up the back—tail to head. If the fish is a dab it will feel decidedly rough. Dabs grow to 1¼ kilos.

RAYS AND SKATE. When it comes to identification, no fish cause more confusion. There are twelve varieties of skate common to Britain. Of these I shall deal with six; the others being rare or inhabiting deep water beyond our range.

All rays and skates have a diamond-shaped body with enlarged pectoral fins, commonly called 'wings'.

THORNBACK RAY (*Raja clavata*). The thornback ray is the commonest and most widely distributed. As the name implies, the back is covered in prickles and spines, with large hooked spines along the tail. Found inshore on all types of flat bottom. Handle the tail area with care. Thornbacks can reach 17 kilos.

CUCKOO RAY (*Raja naevus*). The cuckoo ray has a circular black and yellow spot in the middle of the rounded wings. It is covered with small prickles and has a spiny tail. It grows to 2½ kilos.

PAINTED RAY (*Raja microocellata*). The painted ray is found only off Devon, Cornwall, South Wales and Southern Ireland. It has a grey back with white lines. The tail half of the back is smooth while the head is prickly. It attains 6 kilos.

SPOTTED RAY (*Raja montagui*). The spotted ray has a light brown back with black spots. The smooth skin has a few prickles. It is not found in the northern North Sea. It can reach 6 kilos.

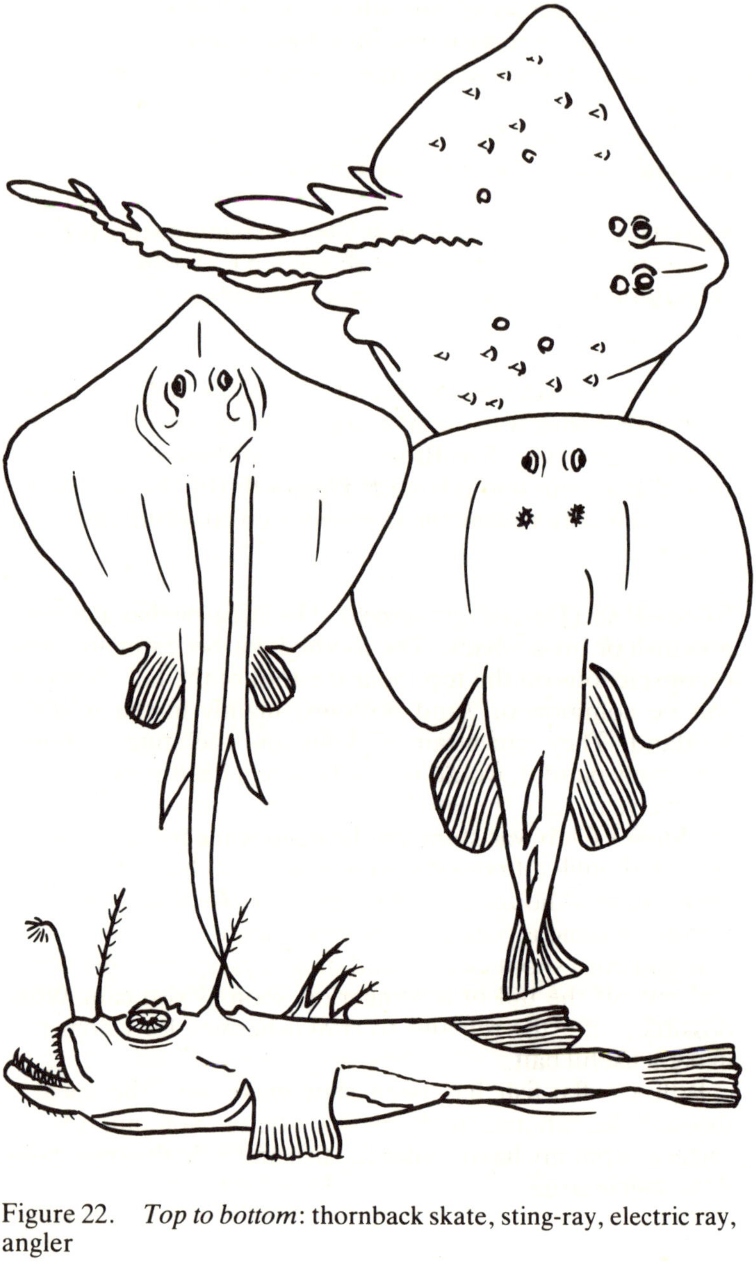

Figure 22. *Top to bottom*: thornback skate, sting-ray, electric ray, angler

Ray wings are good food when skinned, but when there is not an 'R in the month' the flesh has an unpleasant taste of ammonia—in other words they are not worth shooting in the summer.

There are two other rays worthy of mention. Although inedible they can be dangerous if mishandled.

ELECTRIC RAY (*Torpedo nobiliana*). An interesting fish with an electric organ situated in each wing, it is capable of giving a considerable—but not fatal—shock if touched. It is slate grey, banjo-shaped and found on all types of ground. It is rare in the North Sea.

I once shot an electric ray of 23½ kilos at Rame Head, Cornwall during a national competition and experienced no shock whatsoever. But Brian Carlson of the Exe Club had a severe jolt from one taken off Plymouth Breakwater. In my case, I can only assume the shot had been fatal and 'cut off the power'.

STING-RAY (*Dasyatis pastinaca*). The sting-ray has a greyish, greenish or brown back. The toothed, barbed, stinging spine is conspicuous on the top, near the root of the tail. 'Stingers' can be common on sand bottoms, mainly in the south of England. They can attain 27 kilos and the sting, although extremely painful, would not be fatal to a healthy person.

Nine years ago, the late Nick Reuben, a veteran member of the Sussex Club was stung on the hand while fishing at Selsey Bill. Although a first-aid post was at hand, Nick still experienced several hours of acute pain. The usual dressing for a 'stinger' wound is potassium permanganate.

If you must shoot electric and sting-rays, exercise great care and cut off the tail of a 'stinger' as soon as you can. When possible, offer the remains to crab fishermen for whom they make a useful bait.

When a flat-fish has been shot make sure the spear is through the fish and the barbs open before you pull it to the surface. I put my hand under the fish and hold the spearpoint if the fish is large.

ANGLER FISH (*Lophius piscatorius*). The angler fish is

guitar-shaped with a speckled brownish-grey tapering body. It has a loose, smooth skin with flabby, jelly-like flesh. The fish appears to be all head, with an enormous, tooth-filled mouth.

Blending in with a gravel bottom, the angler lies in wait for small fish. When a victim approaches, it waves the first ray of its dorsal fin, situated separately on the snout. The small fish, attracted by this movement, is then sucked into the cavernous mouth—hence the name angler. They have even been known to take birds at the surface. Distributed all around Britain, anglers can reach 40 kilos, 14-kilo fish being quite common.

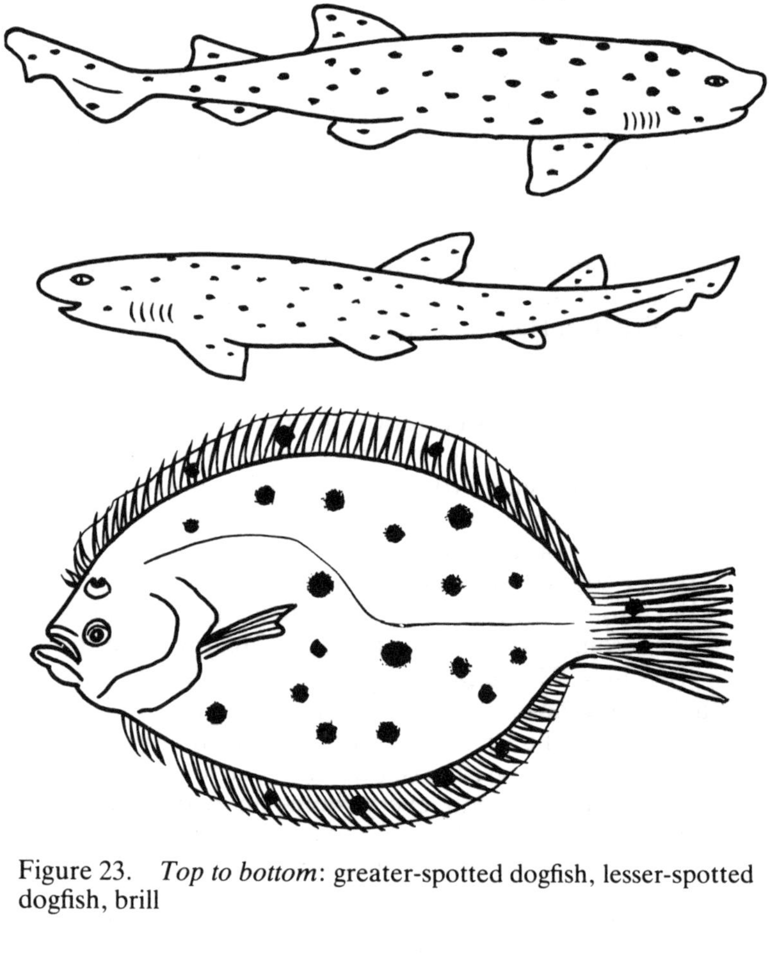

Figure 23. *Top to bottom*: greater-spotted dogfish, lesser-spotted dogfish, brill

The angler fish can be aggressive when speared—I remember a diver at Beesands, Devon, receiving a nasty gash on the finger. At Brixham, I teased a small one of 3½ kilos with a piece of stick I picked up from the bottom. The annoyed fish came at me, crunching along the stick as if it were a piece of celery. Plymouth fisherman Dave Peake recounted an amusing story about an angler, encountered while he was fishing in the corner of Whitsand Bay, Cornwall. Swimming along on the surface, Dave became aware of something tugging at him. Looking behind he saw that a 10-kilo angler was chewing at the end fish of a string of plaice attached to his belt. The fish must have gently grabbed the plaice while Dave was on the bottom.

If hit just behind the eyes, an angler should not give much trouble—avoiding the mouth, get it quickly on your fish-keep (a float is an obvious advantage here). Kill it by severing the spine with your knife.

The tail of the angler is very good eating.

The Monkfish (*Squatina squatina*) is sometimes confused with the angler, but is a separate species altogether, although of similar habits. Its tail is also good eating and is sometimes called 'Brixham Ham' in South Devon.

DOGFISH. Lesser-spotted (*Scyliorhinus caniculus*). This fish has a light brown back with darker spots and a pale belly. It has a shark-like shape (dogfish are smaller members of the selachiian class) with rough, tough skin. The lesser-spotted can weigh up to 4½ kilos.

Greater-spotted (*Scyliorhinus stellaris*). The greater-spotted is sometimes called bull huss. It has a grey background with large round brown spots. Its belly is creamy white and the skin is rough. The greater-spotted can be identified by the nasal flaps on the underside of the head. The flaps do not join across the middle or extend back to the mouth as in the lesser-spotted. The greater-spotted can reach 9 kilos.

Dogfish are common everywhere—in packs and alone under ledges. Aim for the gills and handle with gloves. When skinned, dogfish are good eating and sold under the grand name of 'rock salmon'.

CONGER EEL (*Conger conger*). Normal eel-like appearance. The pectoral fin is pointed and almost reaches the beginning of the dorsal fin; these two features distinguish it from the common eel. It has a brown back, dirty white belly and large doleful eyes and is common, except on the east coast.

Conger fix themselves in ledges and holes on rocky bottoms, wrecks and harbour walls. Sometimes seen free swimming, they feed mainly at night on fish of all kinds.

Armed with a short gun and 7- or 8-mm twin-barbed spear, search the type of ground mentioned. Usually only the head will be seen protruding; get as close as you can and aim just in front of the pectoral fin. If you can, position yourself so that the spear will penetrate at right-angles to the head—this makes it difficult for the fish to retreat back into its refuge. A spear placed centrally through the head, from above, is also effective. As soon as the fish is hit, push the spear well in and start to pull the fish out. You may have to make a lot of dives if the shot was bad or you did not pull hard enough and get him moving right away. It can take a long time to extract a conger if the ledge or hole goes back several metres. Often a fish of 3 kilos puts up more resistance than a larger fish. Sever the spine just behind the head with your knife, avoiding the mouth. Although not aggressive, a conger will bite a carelessly placed hand.

Conger exceed 45 kilos, usually in water of 30 metres and more. The largest conger I have seen landed was a fish of 24 kilos taken by Jimmy Stone of Portland during the 1973 National Competition at Torquay. Inshore, fish of 8 kilos are common everywhere except on the east coast.

Shellfish

I hesitated to include shellfish in a book concerning the pursuit of fish. But, as you search holes and ledges you will encounter crabs and lobsters.

The common edible crab (*Cancer pagurus*) is found throughout the year. The male (cock) is in best condition in the summer, whilst the female (she or hen) is best during the winter. Out of season, crabs tend to be watery. To distinguish between the sexes, turn a crab over, the segmented section in the middle of the underside (known as the purse) is narrow in a male, wide in a female. The male also has much larger pincers. Take a crab by placing the hand across the rear of the shell and gripping the back two legs. If a crab is in a hole, grab the large claws behind the pincers and gently ease or 'rock' it out. Never put your hand over the back of a holed-up crab, the crab will brace its back against the rock trapping your hand.

Lobsters move fast, so have to be grabbed quickly and decisively across the back of the head—a short way back from the eyes. A small gaped hook, 1½ metres long can be a help when trying to dislodge shellfish. Tie a strip of rubber with a largish loop to the handle so that if you want both hands free, the hook can hang from your wrist. Note I say a strip of rubber (inner tubing is ideal). If the hook becomes wedged behind a crab you must, because you are holding your breath, be able to pull your hand free immediately. Line can twist tight or snag behind a watch or glove. Avoid pulling fiercely at the claws of crabs or lobsters as they will shed them to avoid capture. During the summer months spider crabs are plentiful inshore and a large specimen is worth taking. Although not popular here, they are enjoyed in the Channel Islands and in Spain—where most of Britain's catch is sent—and can fetch as much as £8 a kilo.

It is common practice to cook crabs by boiling them whilst alive. This is a needless cruelty. A crab can be quickly and simply killed by laying it on its back and pushing the point of a narrow-bladed knife down into the mandibles (mouth) and piercing the brain. I know of no satisfactory method of killing lobsters without ruining the meat.

Please show a little tact and diplomacy when taking shellfish in areas where they are fished commercially—more than one of us has cause to be thankful for assistance from 'crabbers'.

Following is a month by month guide to give some idea of which fish are inshore and within reach of the spearfisherman and when. No doubt some fishermen will say: "Ah, but I've shot bass in December", as can be the case in the Channel Islands, or, "I've seen shoals of mullet in April". This is of course true. The severity of a winter will dictate fish movements for the early summer, likewise a long hot summer will encourage pelagic fish to stay in our waters longer. What I give is a rough guide for an average year, with average temperatures.

	Bottom Fish	**Round Fish**
JANUARY	Conger, dogfish, angler, sole, dab	Pouting, cod
FEBRUARY	Conger, dogfish, angler, sole, ray, dab	Pouting, cod
MARCH	Conger, dogfish, angler, plaice, flounder, dab	Pouting
APRIL	Conger, dogfish, angler, sole, ray, plaice, flounder, dab	Pouting, wrasse, pollack, coalfish
MAY	Conger, dogfish, angler, sole, ray, plaice, flounder, dab, turbot, brill	Pouting, wrasse, pollack, coalfish
JUNE	Conger, dogfish, angler, sole, ray, plaice, flounder, dab, sting-ray, electric ray, turbot, brill	Pouting, wrasse, pollack, coalfish, bass, mullet, bream, John Dory, mackerel, garfish, red mullet, gurnard
JULY	Conger, dogfish, angler, sole, ray, plaice, flounder, dab, sting-ray, electric ray, turbot, brill	Pouting, wrasse, pollack, coalfish, bass, mullet, bream, John Dory, mackerel, garfish, red mullet, gurnard
AUGUST	Conger, dogfish, angler, sole, ray, plaice, flounder, dab, sting-ray, electric ray, turbot, brill	Pouting, wrasse, pollack, coalfish, bass, mullet, bream, John Dory, mackerel, garfish, red mullet, gurnard
SEPTEMBER	Conger, dogfish, angler, sole, plaice, flounder, dab, sting-ray, electric ray, turbot, brill	Pouting, wrasse, pollack, coalfish, bass, mullet, mackerel, gurnard

	Bottom Fish	**Round Fish**
OCTOBER	Conger, dogfish, angler, sole, plaice, flounder, dab, turbot, brill	Pouting, wrasse, pollack, coalfish, bass, mullet, cod
NOVEMBER	Conger, dogfish, angler, sole, plaice, dab	Pouting, wrasse, pollack, coalfish, bass, mullet, cod
DECEMBER	Conger, dogfish, angler, sole, dab	Pouting, cod

Looking After Your Catch
The correct care of fish after landing is important. Fish deteriorates quickly at normal temperatures and the more so if left in hot sun or the boot of a car. Gut and rinse off your catch as soon as possible; scaling is much easier when fish are fresh and damp than when the scales have become dry and hard. If you intend to fillet and skin a fish then of course there is no point in scaling it. Pollack and pouting are the quickest fish to 'go off', quickly becoming high and soft if caught in the morning and left until the evening. Fish with a full stomach will go off quicker than those with an empty one. Do not leave fish piled up in a bag so those at the bottom get crushed. Lay them in a box in the shade, a piece of wet hessian sacking on top will help keep them cool. On board a boat a bucket of sea water tipped over them now and then is a help. Refrigerate fish as soon as possible.

Scaling. Lay the fish flat and with the sharp edge of a knife at an angle, scrape off the scales working from tail to head rinsing occasionally. Pollack, coalfish and pouting, whilst not having large, tough scales, still need to be scraped.

Gutting. To gut a fish simply slit the stomach from the vent to the gills and withdraw the entire contents, then rinse.

Filleting and Skinning. Again, lay the fish flat, preferably on a board and cut down the side of the backbone working from head to tail. Remove the entire side of the fish. Lay the side skin down and work the knife under the flesh near the tail and, gripping the tail-end skin, push the knife forward cutting as you go. A sharp knife is essential and in this case gutting and scaling is obviously unnecessary.

Immature Fish and the Law

The Ministry of Agriculture, Fisheries and Food, have laid down minimum sizes for the landing and sale of fish and shellfish. These size limits are of course primarily aimed at commercial fishing and the sporting fisherman should regard them as an absolute minimum and set his sights higher. In the early stages when the fire of enthusiasm burns strong, the odd small fish is excusable, but is never something to be proud of; after all, we can see what we intend to shoot.

It is to be hoped that with the increasing use of mid-water trawling techniques, grey mullet will soon be added to the list.

	Centimetres	Equivalent in inches
Cod	30	11.8
Haddock	27	10.6
Hake	30	11.8
Plaice	25	9.8
Witches	28	11.0
Lemon Soles	25	9.8
Soles	24	9.4
Turbot	30	11.8
Brill	30	11.8
Megrims	25	9.8
Whitings	27	10.6
Dabs	15	5.9
Bass	26.4	10.3

Penalties for contravention of these orders include fines not exceeding £1,000 for a first offence.

The Immature Crabs and Lobsters Order 1976
(S.I. No. 305 of 1976) *Landing and Sale of Undersize Crabs and Lobsters.*

Under this Order, which came into force on 15 March 1976, it is an offence to land, sell, expose or offer for sale or be in possession for the purposes of sale of any crabs of

the species *Cancer pagurus* or lobsters (*Homarus gammarus*) which are smaller than the following sizes:
1. Crabs (*Cancer pagurus*)—115 millimetres (4.5″) measured across the broadest part of the back.

Lobsters (*Homarus gammarus*)—80 millimetres (3.2″) measured from the rear of either eye socket to the rear end of the body shell (carapace) along a line parallel to the centre line of the body shell.
2. Any crabs or lobsters below the minimum sizes referred to above which are taken in the course of any fishing operation by means of a fishing boat must be returned to the sea forthwith.
3. Any person contravening this Order is liable to a fine not exceeding £1,000.
4. In addition the byelaws of certain Sea Fisheries Committees further restrict the taking of landing of crabs and lobsters in their Districts, information on those byelaws should be obtained from the Sea Fisheries Committees concerned.
5. For further details reference should be made to the Immature Crabs and Lobsters Order which can be obtained from Her Majesty's Stationery Office or to the nearest Fisheries Office of the Ministry of Agriculture, Fisheries and Food.

It is also an offence to take egg-bearing (berried) lobsters and soft-shelled or berried crabs.

There are no size limits on the rather rare crawfish (*Palinuris vulgaris*) or spider crabs (*Macropodia longirostris*), although moves are afoot regarding spiders.

The Salmon and Freshwater Fisheries Act of 1923 (Section 1) prohibits the taking of salmon, trout or freshwater fish with a spear or similar instrument. So, I am afraid that any ideas of freshwater spearfishing are out.

Sea Temperatures

Water temperature effects fish movements, and the fisherman's ability to hunt effectively. In very cold water the still or slow moving approach for round fish soon brings on the shivers, whereas with the constant diving and searching needed for flat-fish the cold is less noticeable. One can, of course, always draw some small consolation from the fact that the sea temperature is always several degrees higher than that of the land.

Below is an inshore surface temperature guide from my own records, taken from 1968–73.

43°–51°F 6.1°–10°C	51°–58°F 10°–14.4°C	58°–65°F 14.4°–18.1°C
December January February March April	May June July November	August September October

These temperatures were taken exclusively in South Devon. Northern waters will be proportionately colder. The south coast (Sussex in particular) is usually warmer during May to August, having greater expanses of shallow water.

Sharks

It would be unfashionable these days not to mention the subject of sharks.

Sharks are occasionally encountered by divers and spearfishermen around our coasts and a number of incidents have been recorded.

On 30 June 1960, the now discontinued *Daily Sketch* newspaper carried a spread about a twenty-year-old girl named Bonny Somerville who speared a 2-metre blue shark five miles off Fowey—apparently her regular pastime.

At Gorran Haven, near Mevagissey, Cornwall, during the summer of 1964 Roger Libby, Stu Charles and Al Rendle saw the fin of a 5-metre basking shark break the surface. The trio decided to try and take it. When the shark was approached and its proportions clearly seen, only Roger decided to fire. The spear of his Champion momentarily held, then pulled out and the shark continued, unconcerned, on its way.

During hot weather, basking sharks are an almost common sight off west country shores and although harmless, plankton

15. Pete Babbage with a fine Dorset bass

16. Mullet from shallow water in Torbay. Best fish is 1.815 kilos

17. A 5-kilo pollack and (bottom) a British Record red gurnard and another relatively small pollack. Hybrid gun is a broom handle fitted to a commercially made butt

18. British team member Brian Carlson with a 6.520-kilo cod, taken during the 1973 National Competition at Selsey Bill, Sussex

19. Twin plaice of 1.930 kilos. Note correct spear penetration—just behind the head

20. The cavernous mouth of an 18-kilo angler fish, taken in April

21. International Tony Rose with a 12.698-kilo conger, taken near Brixham, Devon

22. A satisfying mixed bag: bass, mullet, plaice and a crab

23. Competitors weighing-in their catches at the 1976 National Competition at St Albans, Dorset

24. Total catch at the 1972 Channel Island Open Competition at Grève De Lecq, Jersey

25. The mullet and its relatives are found in almost all the waters of the world

eaters their size always creates a stir. Late one evening I was swimming back to my starting point under the high sandstone cliffs near Teignmouth in Devon; the sun had set and in the shadow, the sea bed had taken on a sombre, gloomy appearance. Beneath me a kelp bed began to materialize in the dimness and gently swaying among the topmost fonds was a long black shape with a large triangular fin. Swimming closer, I was relieved to find it was only the headless remains of a large 'basker' that had probably become entangled in a moored net, and had been killed and dumped. Just a year ago a 5-metre shark followed the diving boat I was aboard for ten minutes before submerging completely and moving off. Some anglers who had seen the fish from the pier we had just departed from, later swore it was a thresher on account of the high tail fin.

In June 1971, Jim Johnson of the Aldershot Dolphins Diving Club, was snorkel diving from the beach at Beesands, Devon. Fifty metres off shore a shark about 3 metres in length appeared, swam ahead, then turned and came at him. Although terrified, Jim poked the shark, hard on the snout, with his crab hook. After circling for a while the shark made off and Jim finned rapidly for the beach. He believes the shark was a mako, a known man-eater in foreign waters. Over the years I have spent hours diving and spearfishing the Beesands area, but have never seen a shark, and to my knowledge, neither has anyone else.

A good (or bad!) year for sharks was 1971. Fishing off Portland Bill, Dorset, Jimmy Stone, then a member of the Weymouth Club, rounded a rock to come face to face with an estimated 60-kilo shark that, unconcerned, swam past him. Jimmy believed the fish to be a porbeagle, another dangerous variety. Also at Portland, a then new recruit to the Weymouth Club, Barry Axford, had a similar experience.

At the Eddystone reef, 13 miles off Plymouth, where baskers have frequently been encountered, Dave Peake and a friend decided to leave the water after a close encounter with a 2½ metre mako or porbeagle. Although the fish did not menace them, it came a bit too close for comfort.

During the 1973 National Competition at Anvil Point near Swanage, Alan Mills shot a conger. As he was pulling the fish towards him a small shark made several passes at it. Alan put the eel ashore on some nearby rocks and decided to try to take the shark, but on entering the water found it had disappeared.

In 1976 an angler, boat-fishing out from Padstow on the north Cornish coast caught a record 210-kilo porbeagle, a mile off shore in an area known to be frequented by sharks. In July of the following year, Tony Rose and I fished close to the area after swimming from the shore. Fishing in water of 20-metre visibility we took bass and some big pollack, but no sharks were seen (fortunately or not, I am not sure!). Since that day, Tony accompanied by Pete Babbage, has visited 'spot X' a number of times, again taking pollack but there has been no sign of sharks.

During the 1979 Irish Championship, fished at Kilkee, in atrocious conditions, Tony Rose had a large porbeagle pass him (again apparently unconcerned) as he descended to a reef. The incident had little effect and Tony went on to take second place to team mate, Pete Hogan.

From the foregoing the reader may be excused for thinking that perhaps spearfishing is not really for him after all, but in reality the chance of meeting (never mind being attacked by) a shark in British waters, unless of course you made persistent efforts to find them in Cornish waters, are very slim. I would venture to say that Dennis Canniford's record 10.889-kilo blue shark, taken at Looe in 1955 would be an easy record to beat if one put enough thought and time to it. Our friends abroad and in Australia in particular, appear to shoot sharks with about as much concern as we shoot flounders. But I would hesitate to recommend the activity in British waters where lower visibility, non-familiarity with shark habits and inexperience in facing them could prove disastrous.

I have often seen porbeagles and blues on the fish market at Brixham where there is a ready sale for them. The 210-kilo porbeagle mentioned earlier ended up somewhat ingloriously in a north-country fish restaurant where two lady diners confirmed its culinary qualities to a television interviewer. Although not utilized on a large scale in Britain, sharks have many valuable by-products apart from food.

Last season while fishing the Eddystone, Alan Mills had an amusing incident, this time with a large bull seal. Alan had just shot a mullet when he felt a large movement in the water, very close to him. The seal kept hounding him and would not be frightened off, so Alan had to abandon fishing. He says he had the distinct impression he was intruding on the seal's own spot. Most of us have seen seals and they normally give a friendly impression and are beautiful to observe.

7

COMPETITIVE FISHING

Organized competitions took place in Spain as early as 1942 while the first French Championship was organized by Marcel Isy-Schwart in August 1946. It attracted over fifty competitors, one of whom, Louis Lehoux, brought in a 2-metre shark! Three years later, Luigi Stuart Tovini won the first Italian National Championship at Gorgona.

1954. In 1954 a European sportfishing body, the Confederation Internationale de Pêche Sportive, based in Rome, organized the first International Championship at Sestri Levante, Italy, (the event attracting thirty-five competitors from six nations). Gianni Roghi, an Italian, took the individual title, and Spain were top team.

1958. Britain's first participation in the world event came in August 1958 at Sesimbra, Portugal. The team of Albert Hayden (London E.), Team Manager, Brud Martin (Plymouth), Brian Stidwell (Bournemouth), Mike Davies (Brighton), Don Hall (London E.), and Lofty Standing (London E.) simply could not match the experienced opposition. France took the first two individual places and were consequently winning team. The winner was the great Jules Corman, whose catch included a 38-kilo corvina as long as himself. He was sadly to die at Malta the following year. Sixty-eight competitors came from twelve nations.

At the C.I.P.S. Congress held at Brussels in September 1958, the delegates decided to form a World Federation of diving clubs, to be called Confédération Mondiale des Activités Subaquatiques (C.M.A.S.). Its aims were to be the development of underwater activities and sport. International spearfishing competitions would be run by a sports committee and according to C.M.A.S. rules. At Monaco, on 10 January 1959 delegates from fifteen countries formally founded

C.M.A.S. That number has now increased to fifty-one countries.

1959. To return to the World Championships, 1959 saw Malta as the venue. Representing Britain were Keith Pearn, Derrick Baynham, Tony Buxton, Jack Wright with David Oliver as reserve; team manager was Ted Wells from Bournemouth. Of the nineteen countries, Britain finished twelfth—quite creditable if one considers the strength of the opposition. Terry Lentz, with 53 kilos of fish, gave the U.S.A. its only world title to date, although in the following events, the Americans have been consistently well placed. The competition was marred by a number of accidents. Two competitors, Corman (France) and Ramalhète (Portugal) lost their lives and Falzon (Malta) blacked out but was rescued and taken to hospital. An aqualung diver taking photographs also lost his life.

1960. The Aeolian Islands, north of Sicily was chosen for the 1960 Championship. Bruno Hermanny of Brazil won the first of his two world titles in a deep-diving competition; not surprisingly, Italy won the team section. The British team of Reg Vallintine, Jack Wright and Derrick Baynham with Jimmy Hamlyn as manager had to be content with fourteenth place out of the nineteen nations. This championship saw the adoption of three- instead of four-man teams.

1961. At Almeria, Spain, the 1961 championship was of course a runaway victory for the Spanish team. Their total catch weighed 419 kilogrammes compared to 267 kilogrammes for second-placed France. Individual winner was the legendary Juan Gomis, while José Noguera, another long-established Spanish fisherman, was second, and is, like Gomis, still fishing at the time of writing. Britain's Mike Davies (Manager), Derrick Baynham and Bill Tuxworth finished seventeenth and, like most of the other twenty-eight teams, had to bow to the Spaniard's superior knowledge of the area. I think it worth mentioning at this point the extraordinary record of the Italian, Claudio Ripa. From Sesimbra to Almeria he had achieved a second and three third places in world competitions, but first was always to allude him.

1963. Rio de Janeiro, Brazil, was the exotic location for the

1963 Championship and Davey Jones and Mick Barnes (Weymouth), and Roy Moyse from Jersey made the long journey to represent Britain. They faced the problems of acclimatization after the long journey, as well as the different food, uncomfortable climatic conditions, i.e. very hot land temperature, but freezing cold sea and numerous poisonous sea urchins. Davey brushed against some of the urchins and suffered considerable discomfort. France was the victor, but local man, Bruno Hermanny, best individual. Britain came eleventh with Mick Barnes taking the largest mutton fish.

1965. In international events of the '50s and '60s, Britain had achieved little significant success with one very notable exception. At Moorea Island, Tahiti, in the 1965 Championship, the British team of Wilson Dagger (Weymouth), Terry Thomas (Weymouth) and Terry Woodford (Bournemouth) gained fourth place—the highest placed European team—fishing in waters and for fish totally new to them. Wilson in seventh place individually was the highest placed European entrant and his performance at that time was the best ever by a Briton in the World Championships. There were thirty competitors from eleven nations. Rather surprisingly, Australian, Ron Taylor, won with a large fish taken at the last minute. Tahitians Tapu, Colas and Arai won the team prize for France.

1967. Cuba was host to the 1967 competition. The British team of Wilson Dagger and Colin House (Weymouth), Bob Tanner (Southsea) and manager, Mike Davies, were dogged by bad luck and injuries, but managed eleventh place to Cuba. One of the world's greatest fishermen, Jean Tapu, of the French team was best of thirty competitors, taking 250 fish to win the individual title.

1969. The Aeolian Islands were the setting once again for the 1969 Championship. Owing to an administrative mix-up over boats, the first day was cancelled after the eighty-five competitors had been up since 4 a.m. In the one day's fishing left, Britain took nineteenth place in a six and a half hour competition at Salina. The result was put down to low morale, lack of funds, general inexperience, and the poor organization. The team was Terry Thomas, Wally Pack (Sussex), Wilson Dagger, Bob Tanner, Andy Smith (reserve) and Colin

Macleod (manager). Wally was highest placed Britain at thirty-eighth. Massimo Scarpati and Italy were victors with Italians also second and third individually.

1970. The first international event held in British waters, the North European Championships, took place at Plymouth on 28 August 1970 and the British team naturally had high hopes. In the event it proved a benefit for France who took first, third and fourth individual places and were top team. Jean-Baptiste Esclapez was the easy winner. Best placed Briton was Colin House in fifth place; Britain was fourth team.

1971. The cold (50° F) waters of Chile greeted competitors for the 1971 World Championships. In the waters, chilled by the Humboldt Current, fish known as sea-wolves, snatched catches from floats during practice sessions. Bob Milverton (Weymouth), Terry Thomas and Wally Pack, gained 132,100 points to give Britain fourteenth place to Chile with 773,900 points. Chilean Raoul Choque was individual winner. British reserve was Alan Mills (Plymouth) and team manager was Colin McLeod, who, during the fishing, timed some of the foreign competitors at 1 minute 20 seconds to 1 minute 40 seconds underwater. Colin maintained that these dives, with around a minute recovery rates, greatly contributed to these fishermen's success. Twenty nations took part.

1972. It was difficult to break the grip of the 'big three'—Italy, Spain and France. Better year-round conditions, sponsorship, fanatical dedication and the all important fact that the events were invariably held in their home waters, strengthened the continental hold.

Then, in September 1972, the British team of Wally Pack, Alan Mills and Dave Heaphy (Sussex), and now managed by Gerry Weedon (Sussex) gained third place in the European Championships at the Isle of Man. Mills, Heaphy and Pack being sixth, seventh and eighth respectively. France and the Tahitian, Francis Nanai, took the top honours.

At the World Championships of 1973, held at Cadaques, Spain, Britain finished fourth, Wally Pack being fifth individually, the highest place a Briton had yet achieved.

On the first day of the two-day competition, Wally had held second place, but not surprisingly, Spain finished top of the eighteen nations with José Amengual.

The following year at Kilkee, County Clare, Ireland, Amengual became European Champion, but Britain won the team event. Dave Heaphy was third, Alan Mills fourth and Pete Crawford (Exe) seventh. Eric Smith of Sussex was reserve. British spearfishermen had at last won a major event.

1975. In 1975, South America again played host to the World Championships which were held at Paracas, Peru. Britain, with a team consisting of Dave Heaphy, Pete Crawford, Brian Carlson (Exe) and Eric Smith, Reserve, finished seventh, despite an incredible performance by team captain, Pete Crawford. On the second day, Pete took 176 fish (1 fish every 2½ minutes) to set a new World Championship record, and yet he still finished nineth. Once again, the host nation took the team prize with Esclapez of France becoming individual champion.

British spearfishermen, with the then team manager, Gerry Weedon, were becoming a force to be reckoned with in world competition.

1977. At the 1977 A.G.M. of the B.S-A.C.'s National Spearfishing Committee, Gerry Weedon, after considerable success as team manager, decided to stand down. Ron Jacobs of Weymouth was the obvious choice to replace Gerry, having been assistant manager for the previous two years. He had taken teams to minor international events in the Mediterranean, in particular the yearly event at Menorca.

In the July of that year Ron took the team of Pete Crawford, Brian Carlson, Wally Pack and Tony Rose (Exe) to Ustica, near Sicily for the European Championships. Against the almost impossible task of defeating the Italians in their home waters, Britain came fifth; Claudio Martinuzzi and the Italian team winning.

1979. At the time of writing, preparations are in hand for the next World Championships, location as yet undecided.

Our first British National Spearfishing Championship was held at Newton Ferrers, Devon, on August Bank Holiday Sunday 1958. Colin Anderson of Southsea came out best of the forty competitors. In those days, one competition decided the British Champion.

In 1968 it was decided that six or seven competitions should be held, each one in a different location as this would give each man the chance to fish at least one competition in his own area and would produce a fairer, more realistic result. At each event the man with the heaviest catch is awarded one hundred per cent; the points gained by the other catches are worked out as a percentage of the winners. At the end of the season, the man with the highest percentage is champion, the same applying in the team section. Teams for international events are based on these results, taken over two years. The top ten attend training sessions and a team of three with one reserve is selected (see the end of the chapter for the complete home competition rules and points system).

The British home competitions are controlled by the B.S-A.C. National Spearfishing Committee and are held at venues from Cornwall to Yorkshire, but mainly Devon, Dorset, Sussex and Hampshire.

There is an open event held in the Channel Islands every summer, Jersey and Guernsey alternately. Conditions are usually good and prizes include guns, watches and other items of equipment. The Irish Open is held every year, usually at Valentia. Anyone can enter these competitions for a fee of up to £5.

Competitive fishing and the travelling involved may not at first appeal to the beginner, but there are a number of advantages. The chance to visit areas of great diversity and meet other fishermen, and the possibility of winning useful prizes and attractive trophies. Competitors can keep the fish they catch if they so wish, and most do, but the organizers have the responsibility for the useful disposal of any fish unwanted. At the end of the day there is a social event and prizegiving.

Competition Equipment and Preparation

No additional equipment is required for competitive spear-fishing, but it is a good idea to carry on your float a spare spear (changing a spear is made quick and simple if the line is threaded through the hole at the end of the barrel and a simple slip-knot tied (Inset Fig. 3 Top), and if you use a rubber-powered gun a set of rubbers and two spare wishbones. Alternatively, fit a wishbone to both ends of a set of rubbers and wear like a necklace. Some fishermen take two guns of different lengths. Sometimes it may be necessary to carry your catch a long distance back to the designated starting point so most men keep a net bag on their float; fish are more easily carried in a net than if left hanging from a fish-keep where they may break off and be lost.

At most competitions a fair amount of swimming is required to get to a good area or find a spot that you can have, to yourself. With prolonged swimming, it is not unusual for the backs of the knees to become sore owing to the suit trousers chafing with the continuous bending of the legs. A small amount of Vaseline smeared behind the knees will prevent this.

In hot weather, the plastic dustbin or box mentioned in Chapter 2 should be filled with water and your catch left to soak while awaiting the weigh-in. This will decelerate weight loss through dehydration.

Dehydration also effects the fishermen and, coupled with the call of nature, results in a high loss of body fluids. Have sufficient refreshment available for when you leave the water (some competitors carry a plastic bottle of milk or a mixture of glucose and water, attached to their floats). Food on the morning of a competition should be light, easily digestible and high in calories, such as milk, rice, cereal and sugar. Never eat a heavy meal prior to fishing or enter the water with a completely empty stomach.

The pre-season physical training mentioned in Chapter 4 is most important if you intend to do well in the much harder sphere of competitive fishing. Wherever possible, it is a good plan to 'scout' the competition area beforehand to see what fish are available and where. This should be undertaken within a few days of the actual competition to allow for migratory fish movements. One can locate reefs and 'good ground' so that a plan may be formulated for the competition day. However, competitors are not permitted to carry a gun in a competition area within seven days of the event.

There are also a number of other desirable personal qualities: a placid but perseverant temperament; confidence in your own ability and judgement; knowledge of fish habits and movements so that you may change your tactics accordingly and a simple desire to be better than the next man.

Competition today is very keen, for, at stake are places in teams that may travel to South America, the Pacific, Australia, or anywhere in the Mediterranean. Some teams are sponsored by dive shops and equipment manufacturers. Although competitive fishermen are understandably secretive regarding the whereabouts of fish, most are only too willing to help a keen beginner.

BRITISH CHAMPIONS

1958 Colin Anderson (Southsea)
1959 Denis Canniford (Plymouth)
1960 Jack Wright (Bournemouth)
1961 Davey Jones (Weymouth)
1962 Davey Jones (Weymouth)
1963 Adrian Worley (Southsea)
1964 Terry Thomas (Weymouth)
1965 Mick Barnes (Weymouth)
1966 Mick House (Weymouth)
1967 Stan Beall (Plymouth)
1968 Colin House (Weymouth)
1969 Terry Thomas (Weymouth)
1970 Bob Milverton (Weymouth)
1971 Pete Crawford (Exe)
1972 Wally Pack (Sussex)
1973 Dave Heaphy (Sussex)
1974 Pete Crawford (Exe)
1975 Dave Heaphy (Sussex)
1976 Brian Carlson (Exe)
1977 Pete Crawford (Exe)
1978 Mike Bradshaw (Sussex)
1979 Pete Hogan (Exe)

TEAM CHAMPIONS

1958 Bournemouth B.S-A.C.
1959 Plymouth Underwater Fishing Club
1960 Plymouth Underwater Fishing Club
1961 Associated Divers, Weymouth
1962 Jersey Sub-Aqua Club
1963 Portland and Weymouth B.S-A.C. 'A'
1964 Jersey Sub-Aqua Club
1965 Guernsey Blue Dolphins
1966 Associated Divers Stingrays
1967 Weymouth Makos
1968 Weymouth Makos
1969 Weymouth Makos
1970 Weymouth Sharpitz
1971 Weymouth Makos
1972 Sussex Watersports
1973 Sussex Gamleys
1974 Sussex Gamleys
1975 Sussex Gamleys
1976 Blandford Mares
1977 Blandford Mares
1978 Blandford Mares
1979 Blandford Mares

THE WORLD CHAMPIONSHIPS

Date and Place	*Individual*	*Team*	*G.B. Placing*
1954 Sestri Levante, Italy	Roghi (Italy)	Spain	—
1955 Palma, Majorca	Jannuzzi (Italy)	France	—
1956 Bastia, Corsica	Mairata (Spain)	Spain	—
1957 Mali Losinj, Jugoslavia	Catalani (Italy)	Italy	—

Date and Place	*Individual*	*Team*	*G.B. Placing*
1958 Sesimbra, Portugal	Corman (France)	France	—
1959 Valletta, Malta	Lentz (U.S.A.)	Spain	12th
1960 Palermo, Sicily	Hermanny (Brazil)	Italy	14th
1961 Almeria, Spain	Gomis (Spain)	Spain	17th
1963 Rio De Janeiro, Brazil	Hermanny (Brazil)	France	11th
1965 Moorea, Tahiti	Taylor (Australia)	France	4th
1967 Caya Avolos, Cuba	Tapu (France)	Cuba	11th
1969 Aeolian Islands, Italy	Scarpati (Italy)	Italy	19th
1971 Iquique, Chile	Choque (Chile)	Chile	14th
1973 Cadaques, Spain	Amengual (Spain)	Spain	4th
1975 Paracas, Peru	Esclapez (France)	Brazil	7th

EUROPEAN CHAMPIONSHIPS
(Formerly Afro-European Championships)

Date and Place	*Individual*	*Team*	*G.B. Placing*
1962 Tremiti, Italy	Paladino (Italy)	Italy	—
1964 Tremiti, Italy	Trealeani (Italy)	Italy	9th
1966 Ustica, Italy	Gomis (Spain)	Spain	6th
1968 Majorca, Spain	Gomis (Spain)	Italy	7th
1970 Mali Losinj, Yugoslavia	Atoine (France)	Italy	5th
1972 Isle of Man, Britain	Nanai (France)	France	3rd
1974 Kilkee, Southern Ireland	Amengual (Spain)	Great Britain	1st
1977 Ustica, Italy	Martinuzzi (Italy)	Italy	5th

British Sub-aqua Club

Rules governing National Spearfishing Competitions in Great Britain, November 1979.

All Competitors must be over the age of 15 years[1] and those up to 18 years must have written permission from a parent or guardian on the entrance form provided.

All Competitors must be registered and issued with a competition number by the National Spearfishing Committee.

Any Competitors entering a competition individually will be grouped into teams of three. A Team will consist of three persons and no replacements will be permitted after the start of the competition.

If a competition has to be stopped for any reason, the Organising Committee will decide whether or not

[1]There is no reason why a capable youngster, under experienced supervision, should not start to fish much younger. This rule covers the harder field of competition, where conditions often require a high degree of experience.

sufficient time has elapsed since the start to constitute a valid Competition, but the time elapsed must be at least half that originally intended as the duration of the Competition.

The National Spearfishing Committee Safety Officer shall inspect safety arrangements on the day of a national competition prior to the start. If he is dissatisfied he will report his findings to all members of the National Spearfishing Committee present and they shall then declare the Competition void and post a notice at the briefing to this effect.

No competition will be approved unless paragraphs (b), (c), (d) and (g), Sections 1 and 2 of the Competition Code for organisers have been complied with.

Competition Organisers must designate a starting and finishing area at the water's edge. This will be called the Designated Starting Area (D.S.A.).

1. All Competitors must start at the D.S.A. in full Spearfishing equipment.
2. Competitors may make for their selected site by walking, running or swimming, immediately after the start of the competition.
3. No Competitor will be allowed to start from a Boat, or have the use of any Boat other than that allowed by the Competition Organisers.
4. The Competitor must return himself and his catch to the D.S.A. by his own physical efforts before the official finishing time. He should sign out as soon as possible.
5. Any Competitor arriving back at the D.S.A. after the official finishing time will be penalised as follows: for up to 10 minutes after the end his score will be halved. After 10 minutes he will be Disqualified. Any fish brought in by a competitor who is disqualified will not be eligible for any Trophy or Prize.
6. It is not permitted to use any means to catch Fish other than by knife, handspear or a spear expelled by a gun using compressed air, a spring or rubber. No cartridge or expellable gas guns may be used. Guns must not be loaded on a beach or in a boat and must be unloaded before leaving the water.

7. Any Diver, found or proved to be in a designated competition area during the 7 days prior to a Competition will not be eligible to compete in that event.
8. Competition organisers should send out at least one month in advance of their Competition to all competing clubs, details of their intended Competition Area including any alternatives and areas that will be out of bounds. These areas will be clearly described and will be known as the Designated Competition Area.
9. That anyone fishing outside the D.C.A. during a Competition will be disqualified from that Competition and the two ensuing Competitions.
10. Whilst taking part in a Competition all Competitors must tow an inflated marker buoy size between 8 and 18 inches across. Competitors must at all times be within 60 feet of their buoy (measured across the surface). The specification of the Marker Buoy is as follows:

A Patent Manufactured Buoy;
A Full Size Football;
A one gallon plastic container;
The colour should be Flame Orange or Red/White.

11. The Competitor must be immersed in the water at the time of spearing any fish.
12. No breathing apparatus may be used other than a snorkel.
13. A Competitor may come ashore as often as he wishes but can not use any means of Transport to get to or from any part of the Competition area, or back to the D.S.A. other than that provided by the Organisers.
14. A Competitor may not normally approach within 25 ft of any other Competitor or spear a fish within that radius of another Competitor without his permission. If he helps another Competitor to catch a fish in any way, he will be entitled to 50% of the points for that fish.
15. No lures of any description are permitted to attract fish.
16. A Competitor helping another in the case of injury or exhaustion will be entitled to 50% of the other's catch at that time.

17. The passing of fish in any way will disqualify both the persons concerned and their team(s).

18. To qualify a fish must be caught in the D.C.A. and within the time limits for the Competition. It must weigh 500 grammes or over. It may be weighed in at any time by the Official appointed for that duty, but if the Competitor signs out after the Competition ends, Rule 5, paragraph (e) will apply.

19. A Balance Scale will be used to establish that a Fish is heavy enough to qualify.

20. Any Competitor, not being a current member of the B.S-A.C., or who is unable to produce his current membership receipt when asked will be required to pay an extra 50p to enter a Competition. This will be collected by the Organisers and passed on to the National Spearfishing Committee to be paid into their funds.

21. No equipment other than Basic Spearfishing equipment may be used unless sanctioned by the Competition organisers.

22. The Competition organisers may alter or add to these Rules if they feel that it is necessary for the particular area where the Competition is being held. Any such alteration or addition must have the prior approval of the National Spearfishing Committee.

23. The points system for all National Spearfishing Competitions is set out in a separate list attached to these Rules.

24. RESULTS AND OBJECTIONS. The Competition Results should be on display for one hour prior to the Prizegiving for each event. Any persons wishing to lodge a complaint must do so in writing at least half an hour before the Prizegiving.

25. Any Breach of these Rules will mean absolute disqualification.

26. Scoring System and minimum Weight for Competitions.

Minimum Weight.	Bass 1,000 grammes, all other fish 500 grammes.

Round Fish	1,000 point for catching Fish + 1 point per gramme weight (No maximum).
Flat and Bottom Fish	500 points for catching fish + ½-point per gramme weight. Maximum points per fish: 2,500.

B.S-A.C. National Spearfishing Committee Competition Code

A code for organisers of, and competitors in, national competitions
(November 1979).

(a) Full information on the competition must be sent to all branches at least FOUR WEEKS prior to the event.
(b) Red Cross, St John's Ambulance or equivalent safety service must be present at the competition venue.
(c) The competition should be organised by a committee of at least 3 members, one non-competitor who must be responsible for safety precautions.
(d) There must be not less than three safety boats, one of which must be capable of staying out in the competition area in case of bad weather, to recall or collect divers.
(e) All safety boats should have a B.S-A.C. 3rd class (or equivalent) diver aboard and fly the ALPHA flag. The operators of the boats must have knowledge of first aid and the divers' signals.
(f) Shore lookouts should be posted at vantage points around the competition area.
(g) The following organisations and individuals must be notified that a spearfishing competition is to take place:

1. Local R.N.L.I. and inshore rescue group.
2. Local coastguard.
3. Local police.
4. Local harbourmaster (where applicable).
5. Local helicopter rescue base.
6. Local boating, sailing and angling clubs.

(h) Trophies and prizes are to be awarded as follows:

1. Trophies for 1st, 2nd and 3rd teams.
2. Trophies and/or prizes for 1st to 10th individuals.
3. Trophies for: (a) Heaviest flat or bottom fish.
   (b) Heaviest round fish.

(c) Heaviest conger.
(d) Specimen fish—this trophy to be awarded for the best percentage of the current British record weight.

(i) A balance sheet for the competition must be sent to the National Committee Treasurer TWO WEEKS after the competition.

(j) Where possible, all fish of the same SPECIES are to be weighed in bulk. Specimen fish may be weighed separately.

(k) A list of results must be displayed one hour prior to the prizegiving.

(l) The competition organisers may, with the approval of the National Committee add to or alter the competition rules if they feel it is necessary for the particular area where the competition is being held. All competitors must be made aware of any changes in the rules.

(m) WRASSE can be included at the discretion of the competition organisers but competitors must be notified 1 MONTH prior to the competition date.

(n) The National Committee's Adjudicating Committee will be present at all competitions to deal with complaints regarding competitors or the organisers. All complaints must be presented in writing.

(o) Organisers should arrange for the useful disposal of all fish that the competitors do not wish to retain.

(p) Competition organisers must forward a copy of the final results to the National Spearfishing Committee for ratification.

(q) Any spearfisherman or group of spearfishermen causing damage to property or committing acts to the detriment of spearfishing will be answerable to the National Spearfishing Committee. Proven misdemeanours could result in offenders being banned from participating in up to three consecutive national competitions.

(r) Clubs or competition organisers who fail to comply with this code as laid down by the National Spearfishing Committee may not be permitted to hold another competition in the following year.

8

FISHING ABROAD

When you have become proficient in fishing British waters, it is natural to think of the possibilities of fishing in foreign seas with their promises of clear, warm water and different, larger fish. When planning a fishing holiday, a number of important matters must be looked into.

Regulations

Some countries have total bans on spearfishing, whilst others have strictly enforced regulations regarding equipment, weight of fish to be taken, and the time of day fishing is permissible. Most continental countries require you to have a permit or licence, some a medical certificate and/or diving qualification. To avoid problems, write to the national club of the country you intend to visit and ask for full details of the current regulations before finally booking the trip. Some tourist offices issue free brochures showing the best areas for fishing and the type of fish available.

The useful disposal of your catch is as important abroad as it is at home. Do not shoot fish and leave them to rot on the beach—that is the hallmark of the tourist and not the true, responsible, spearfisherman. Take only fish that you can use yourself (this will depend of course on your accommodation arrangements), or can give to the people with whom you are staying. Fish can be exchanged for goods or in payment for the services of boatmen. But, remember that in many cases it is illegal to sell fish taken by spearfishing methods or if you are not a registered fisherman of the particular country. For the transportation of equipment the cost and availability of hire cars is a matter to consider. And in these times changing political situations should be heeded.

Equipment

The normal equipment as used at home is adequate in most cases, but include in your kit: spare 7- or 8-mm spears and some heavy twin-barbed heads (detachable type if very large fish are anticipated), 30 metres of floating 5-mm courlene or polypropalene float-line, a torch, some 3-mm spear-line and a selection of spares such as straps, wishbones and rubbers. Be sure the gun you take is powerful enough for the fish you are likely to meet. Fish of over 20 kilos require a double rubber or air-gun of 130 cm in length. Airlines prefer to carry air guns empty of air, so do not forget the pump and some oil.

Suits

In waters of over 70° F a suit jacket and swimming trunks, or a 'shortie' suit is sufficient. A shortie suit is the same as a full-length suit, except that the arms end at the elbows, and the legs at the knees. They are made in 3- or 4-mm material. But from the point of view of protection from rocks or coral a 3- or 4-mm full suit is still worn by most fishermen unless the water is so warm as to make it unbearable.

Techniques

Fish can be divided into three types, each requiring different techniques:

1. *Small to medium size bottom and mid-water fish*. This covers our own British type of fishing and with fish of similar habits is available throughout the world.

2. *Large open-water fish*. Fishing for large pelagic fish such as amberjack and tuna is practised mainly in Australia, New Zealand and the Americas. Such powerful fish as these cannot be controlled with the usual short length of line with the gun held in the hand. At attempt to do so would result in the gun being pulled from the grasp and lost. Instead, one end of a strong 100-metre 'tethering line' is tied to a large inner tube or buoy (Fig. 28A2); the other end tied to the spear (large barbs or detachable head). When the fish is hit it rushes off dragging the buoy, leaving the fisherman free to surface for air, get into a boat and, if necessary, play the fish from there. In New Zealand fishermen use a large reel attached to the gun (Fig. 27C) and control the fish rather like an angler. But for very

powerful fish the first method, what Americans call 'break-away gear' is the safest. In waters where there may be obstructions, such as wreckage, 4 metres of steel cable—such as used for shark-angling traces—is attached to the spear; the float-line is tied to a swivel at the other end. This reduces the chance of the line being worn through in the event of a snag. Another American method for obstructed waters is 4 metres of cable attached to the spear; at the other end a small float and short length of rope. The piece of rope is held as the spear is fired and the fishermen 'rides' the fish until it tires (Fig. 28A3). Except in shallow water, this method would require the use of an aqualung.

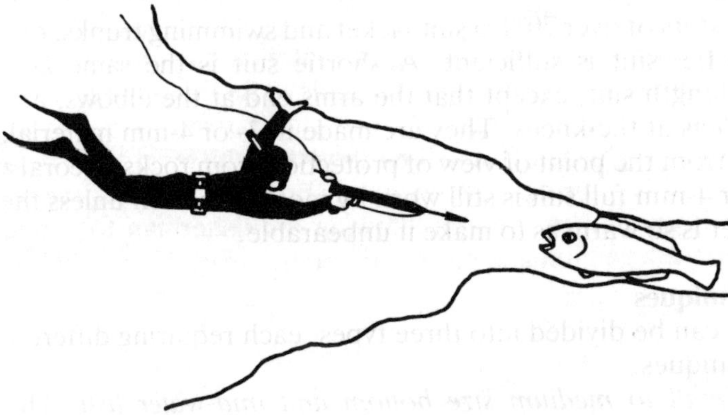

Figure 24. The approach when cave or hole fishing

3. *Small to large territorial and cave-dwelling fish*. This style of fishing has become a fine art in the Mediterranean and its masters are the French, Italians and Spanish. Fish such as grouper, bream and corb spend much of their time in caves and under ledges and have to be sought there (Fig. 24). As such confined places are dimly lit, a torch is indispensable and knee-pads save wear on the suit (Fig. 25). When grouper are hit they retreat back into the cave and a gaff (Fig. 26) can help to dislodge them. The gaff is made from steel rod (about 10 mm thick) with about 10 cm gape. When the fish has been drawn within reach, the traditional continental method is to hold it by putting thumb and index finger in the eyes; this having a paralysing effect. Of course it is best to try to hold the

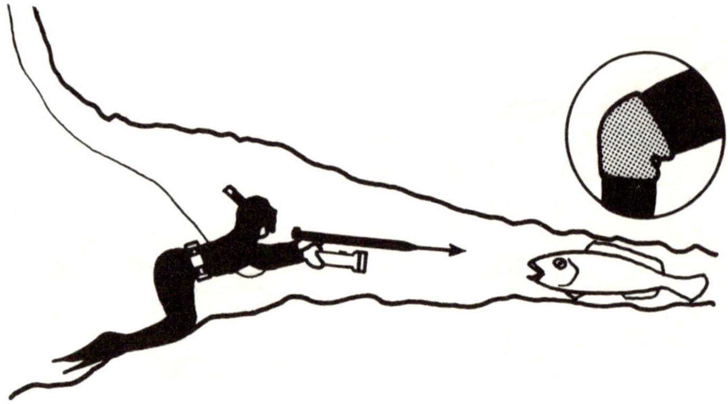

Figure 25. Use of torch. *Inset*—knee-pads

fish before it has a chance to retreat well back into its hole, thus saving a lot of time and trouble. The float-line is tied to the ring on the gun (Fig. 28A1) or, alternatively, a reel is worn on the weight-belt (French method). In the event of it being impossible to bring a fish up on one breath, the end of the reel line is clipped to the gun allowing the fisherman to surface whilst still retaining contact with the fish (Fig. 27, A and B).

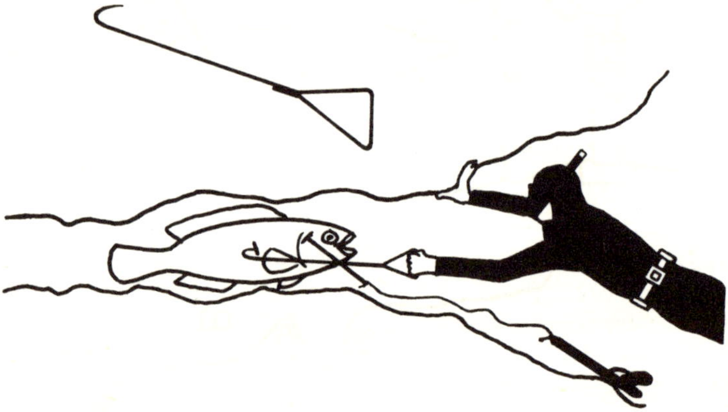

Figure 26. The gaff used to extricate a fish that has wedged itself in a hole

Over the years, the amount of fishing practised in the Mediterranean has in some cases driven grouper into deep (20

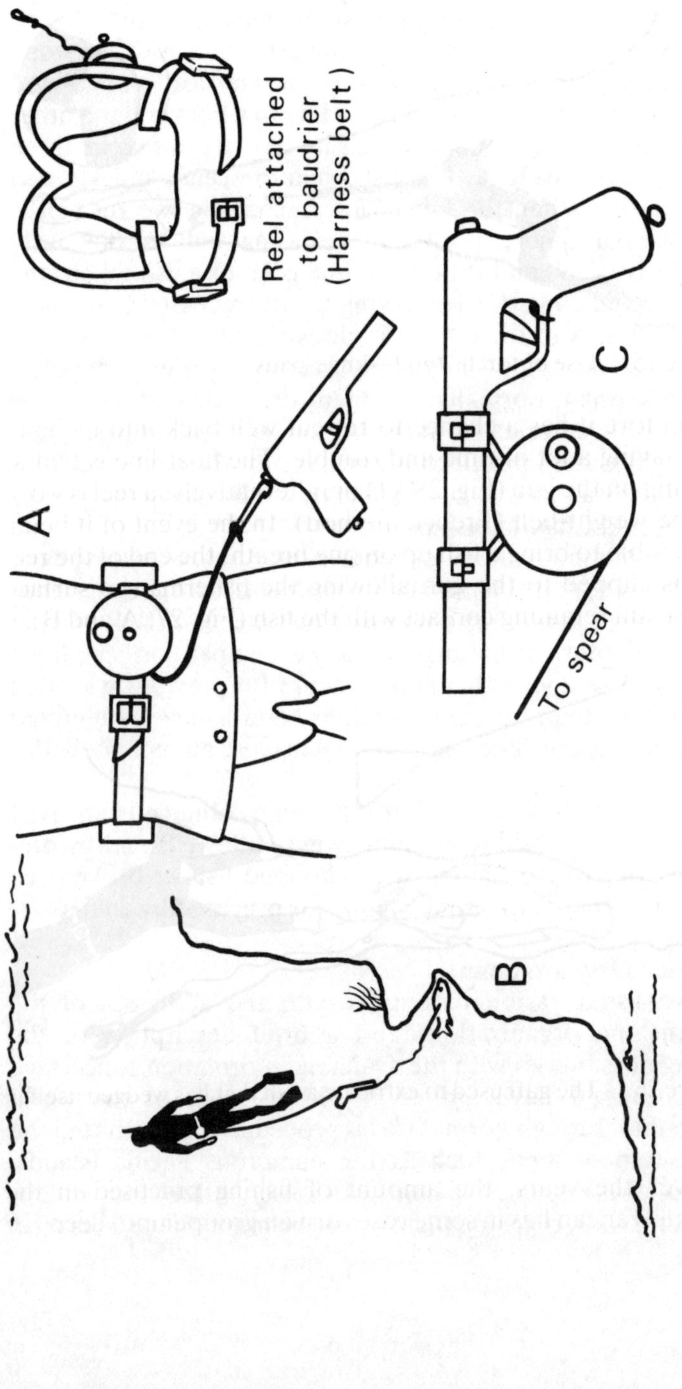

Figure 27. A. Reel on weight-belt with line clipped to gun. B. Fisherman leaves gun and heads for surface, line paying off from reel. C. Reel attached to gun

metres and more) water. To get at these fish has called for a very specialized technique, sometimes referred to as 'bombing' (Fig. 28B)—actually modern versions of the stone tied to a length of rope method of the classical sponge- and pearl-divers. The fisherman ties a line to a float and the other end to his weight-belt, to which he has added two or three kilos of extra weight. The fisherman descends quickly and effortlessly. When the bottom is reached the weight-belt is released (a quick, positively releasing belt is obviously imperative). When his bottom time is up or a fish taken, the ascent is equally effortless owing to the increased buoyancy. A variation is to tie a 4- or 5-kilo weight to a length of line (many use hosepipe—its rigidity making it easier to handle). The fisherman, normally weighted, drops down holding the weight which is released at the bottom or required place; belt or weight is then pulled to the surface for the next dive. This technique was used to good effect by the Brazilians to win the 1970 World Championships.

Both 'bombing' methods require quick, easy-clearing ears, and the weighted belt method in particular, a lot of experience and *through familiarity with one's buoyancy* (or lack of it) at various depths. 'Bombing' is really a competition technique where one is diving to a known depth for previously located fish, rather than random searching, and is *never* attempted unless an experienced companion is in close attendance with a boat.

In addition to 'bombing', results can be obtained in heavily fished areas by fishing at night (where allowed) and by pre-baiting or ground baiting with chopped fish or broken sea urchins, rather in the same manner as practised by anglers.

National Organizations

I have listed various countries with the addresses of the spearfishing organizations and a brief description of the fishing possibilities with the available information concerning regulations. I have limited myself to parts of the world accessible through normal travel procedures and omitted the more remote areas such as the numerous Pacific Islands. While these places would obviously offer tremendous opportunities, reaching them would be more on the lines of an

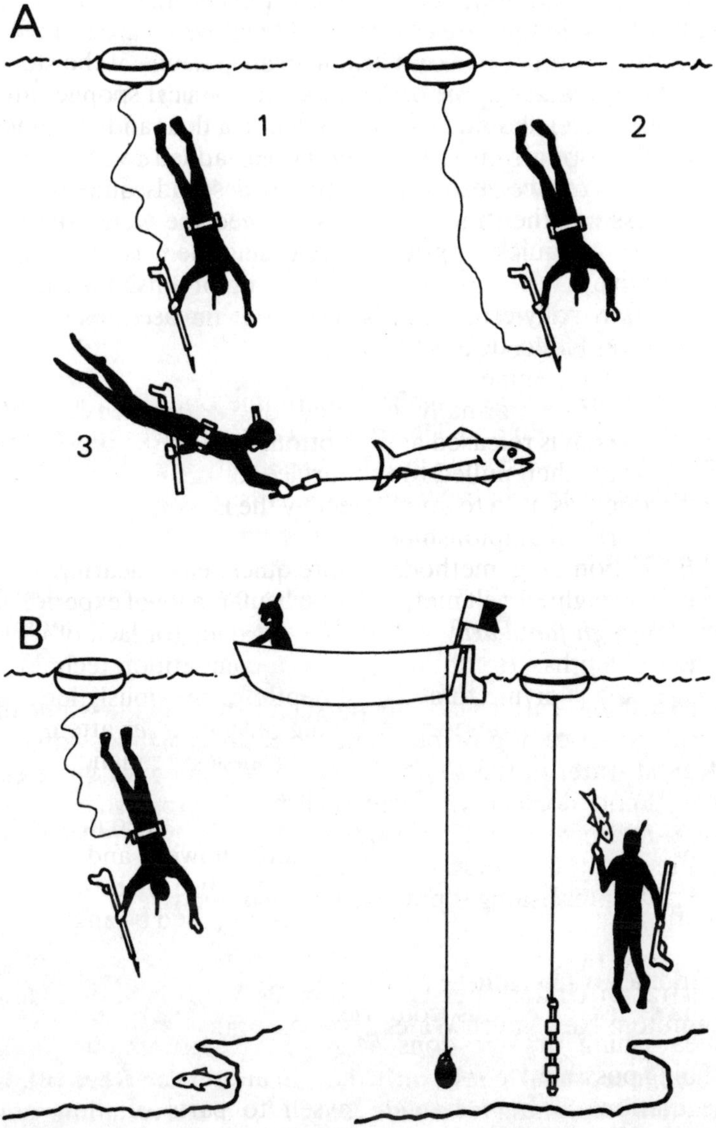

Figure 28. A. Line from float to gun(1), float to spear(2), spear attached to cable and held by fisherman(3). B. 'Bombing'—fisherman dives and surfaces, leaving belt or weight at bottom

extensive expedition, rather than a holiday trip. It must be realized that in the case of restricted areas which are changed from time to time, to avoid fishing in an area where a restriction is in force, the appropriate authority, usually the police or harbourmaster should be contacted on arrival. For those who have the opportunity for regular travel, a copy of the C.M.A.S. Yearbook, available from B.S-A.C. headquarters, will prove most useful.

ALGERIA

Fédération Algerienne de Sauvetage et de Secourisme, 20 Rue du 1er Novembre—Alger

Virtually the entire coastline offers fine opportunities, but between Djidjelli and Tigzirt is best for grouper, bream and corb. In the west, toward Mostaganem, are all kinds of Mediterranean fish, especially large bass.

ARGENTINA

Federacion Argentina de Actividades Subacuaticas, Casilla de Coreo 21, Puerto Madryn, Provincia de Chubut, Argentina

Spearfishing, enthusiastically pursued here as in the whole of South America, is possible along the entire coastline, with the clearest water in the south. Mostly hole fishing for grouper, sea-salmon, dogfish, sar, elephant fish, robalo and shark, in 3- to 30-metre depths. The water is cold—maximum 21° C in summer to 4° C in winter.

Freshwater fishing is practised in lakes and rivers.

AUSTRALIA

Australian Underwater Federation, 24 Victoria Street, New Lambton, New South Wales 2305, Australia

The Queensland coast with the Great Barrier Reef offers tremendous fishing for a wide range of species, including very large grouper (200 kilos plus). New South Wales is a popular area containing large stocks of fish. In southern New South Wales and Tasmania, kelp beds replace the coral reefs of the north and fish life is different in the cooler waters.

The northern part of the west coast is coral with similar fish to the Barrier Reef. The southern west coast is limestone with many caves and plenty of fish. The northern territory is the least interesting area, whilst the south has the highest incidents of shark attacks.

No permit is required for spearfishing, but in South Australia a spear-gun licence is required. Fishing with an aqualung is prohibited. Certain areas of Queensland are reserves where some fish are protected. Rules vary from state to state, so full information should be obtained from the Federation.

BAHAMAS

The Ministry of Agriculture and Fisheries, P.O. Box N3028, Nassau

There is a wide variety of fine fish—amberjack, barracuda, grouper, tuna, tarpon, wahoo, but they are difficult to obtain, owing to legislation. It is illegal to use a spear-gun or any breathing apparatus other than a snorkel for spearfishing. Pole spears and Hawaiian slings only are permitted. Crawfish must not be taken. Spearfishing is prohibited in certain areas, particularly around New Providence. Full details may be obtained from the address above.

BERMUDA

The use of spearguns is totally banned in Bermudan waters; any gun brought in will be impounded. A hand spear may be used, but only one mile or more off shore and not with breathing apparatus. Not more than two fish or any one species may be taken; no more than two lobsters may be taken in any twenty-four-hour period, and none between 1 April and 31 August.

BRAZIL

Confederaçao Brasileira de Deportos, Riva da Alfandega 70, Guanabara, Ciaxa postal, 1078 Rio de Janeiro, Deportes

Brazil offers tremendous spearfishing along its entire coastline, the islands being particularly good. The clearest water is in the north-east. Grouper of 300 kilos have been speared and there are many varieties in the 10-kilo range and liche are also present. The water is generally warm.

Hunting Big Fish by Marcel Isy-Schwart (Burke, 1954) gives an enthralling account of the fishing in the Rio area.

BULGARIA

Fédération Bulgare de sports sous-marins, 48 Bul Christo Botev, Sofia, Bulgaria

Fishing is practised on the rocky or sandy Black Sea coast in good visibility and warm water (May to October). There are no restrictions.

CANADA

Association of Canadian Underwater Councils, 333 River Road, Vanier City, Ontario, KIL 8B9, Canada

Owing to legislation, Canada offers little to the spearfisherman. Although a permit is not required, there are banned species and catch limitations in all the provinces and a total ban on spearfishing in Ontario.

CAYMAN ISLANDS

The coral reefs encircling the islands contain such fish as barracuda, grouper, and snapper. Good areas are within easy reach of the shore. There are plenty of boats and guides available.

Hunting with aqualung is banned and "spearfishermen may take no more than five lobsters and six fish per day". The lobster season runs from 31 July to 1 February.

There is a B.S-A.C. branch on Grand Cayman.

CHILE

Federacion Chilena de Deportes Submarinos y Actividades Subacuaticas, Vicuna Mackenna 44, Casilla 188, Santiago de Chile

Spearfishing is very popular in Chile and its coast offers plenty of fish and many species. Water temperature varies from 20° C in the north to 9° C in the central area. The south down to Punta Arenas is very cold. The sea bed is mostly kelp-covered rocks. Robinson Crusoe Island has clear waters (30 metres visibility) and was the location of the South American Championships in 1964 when competitors from five countries took 1,516 kilos of fish.

An examination by the federation is the only regulation.

COLOMBIA

Federacion Colombiana de Buceo «Por la seguridad en el buceo y un equilibrio ecologico», Piscinas Panamericanas, Apartado Aero 1098, Cali

There is good fishing throughout the year. The best areas are Santa Marta, Los Rosario Islands (shark and barracuda) and San Andres Island.

CUBA

Comision Nacional de Actividades Subacuaticas, Direccion do Organismos Internacionales, Minrex, Habana, Cuba

Spearfishing is very popular and there are centres around the coast. The waters are warm and clear, particularly in the south, with grouper, jack, tarpon and snappers. There are many competitions held with over a thousand teams competing. President Castro is, himself, a keen spearfisherman.

A permit has to be obtained at the National Institute for Tourism (I.N.I.T.).

CYPRUS

Cyprus Sub-Aqua Club, Arch Makarios, 3rd Ave. 75, P.O. Box 4037, Nicosia.

There are the usual run of Mediterranean fish (bass, mullet, bream) and conditions. The north-western coast is reckoned to be best.

There are no restrictions at present, except the use of explosives, but the Department of Fisheries is currently considering regulations regarding fishing with the aqualung.

Equipment is readily available for hire and boats can be hired at all harbours.

Denmark

Dansk Sportsdykker Forbund, Postboks 173, 1005 Copenhagen

Visibility is poor on the west coast, but owing to the large coastline and 500 islands, favourable areas can always be found. The water is cold with best visibility in spring and autumn. There are rocky reefs with cod and flat-fish.

A permit is required, except by Scandinavians. Contact the federation. Fishing can only be carried out with single-pointed spears.

Egypt

The National Skindiving and Underwater Fishing Club, Hurghada Beach, Red Sea Coast, Egypt

The Red Sea coast offers exciting opportunities in warm, clear, coral waters. At Ein Sukhna, spearfishing can be practised "in perfect freedom". The famous area of Hurghada, 385 kilometres south of Suez, has grouper, barracuda, tuna, ling and many others—and of course sharks. The islands of Smaller and Greater Gefton, Shadwan and Jubal opposite Hurghada are also noted fishing grounds. Worth mentioning too, are Ras Ghareb, Al-Qusseir and Safaga. The Mediterranean coast is mainly sand with the odd rocky promontory harbouring bass, mullet, bream, grouper and sometimes tuna and liche. In the neighbourhood of Alexandria noted spots are the Agami peninsula, Sidi-Bishr and Abu Keir.

Finland

Suomen Urkeilusukeltajain Liitto r.y., Topeluikesenkatu 41 a, 00250 Helsinki 25.

Visibility is generally of only 2–3 metres with a mud or sand bottom. May to July are the best months. Spearfishing is popular despite the conditions, with good flat-fishing.

Fishing is not allowed at Aland. A permit from the local Post Office and authorization from the proprietor of the water is required.

FAEROES ISLANDS
Faroese Underwater Federation, Vardagöta 27, 3800 Torshavin.

There is a rugged coastline with huge cliffs. The water is cold—14° C maximum in summer. Visibility in winter is up to 25 metres. The eastern coast is best. Cod, plaice, sole, halibut and sea perch can be found. There are no regulations.

FRANCE
Fédération française d'études et de sports sous-marins, 24 Quai de Rive—Neuve, 13007 Marseille

Fish and conditions on the Atlantic coast are similar to the Channel Islands and Cornwall, with the Brest area being good. The Mediterranean coast offers warm, clear water, but has been heavily fished for forty years by skilled spearfishermen. Experience and good diving ability is required to catch anything of note and the area is not recommended for beginners; the same applies to French Polynesia. The southern part of Corsica and the Marseille area can be good for bass, but a boat is really needed. Best time is September/October as with most of the Mediterranean. There are many regulations—a permit has to be obtained from the office of Maritime Affairs or a membership card from the F.F.E.S.M. One has to be over sixteen years of age. It is prohibited to:

- Fish with an aqualung.
- Use expellable gas or explosive guns.
- Carry aqualung and spearfishing equipment on a boat at the same time.
- Spear fish between sunset and sunrise.
- Spear fish within 150 metres of ships, fishing boats or nets.
- Trap fish in nets.
- Use illuminated traps (torches) for fishing.
- Sell fish.
- Spear shellfish.

Each region also has prohibited zones, so advice must be sought from local clubs. One must also pay heed to size limits.

Despite this terrible burden of regulation, spearfishing is

very popular and France produces some of the world's best fishermen.

GREECE
Hellenic Federation for Underwater Activities and Sports-fishing, Agios Kosmas, Glyfada, Athenes

The popularity of spearfishing and the commercial use of dynamite has made the popular regions profitable only to the most capable fishermen. The remote islands still offer good possibilities, however, for grouper, bass, bream and mullet.

No permits are required, but one must be over eighteen years of age. It is prohibited to:

Fish with an aqualung.
Sell one's catch.
Catch fish less than 150 grammes.
Approach nets or fishing gear.
Fish near beaches where there are bathers.

It is also forbidden to fish the Gulf of Salonica from Piraeus to Sounion.

HAWAII

Bass, big eye, goat fish, parrot fish, amberjack and many more are all to be found. The best areas are Kona coast, Kauai (in the south), Molakai (north), Waianae coast of Oahu (this is where Jack Ackerman took the world record by catching a 58-kilo pompano with an Hawaiian sling), and between Maui and Lanai. Plenty of guides are available.

HONG KONG
Underwater Federation of Hong Kong, G.P.O. 9012, Hong Kong

Best conditions are during spring and summer (mid-April to September) with a maximum water temperature of 27° C. The coastline is rugged with 230 islands, making best areas accessible only by boat. Sharks, barracuda, wrasse and parrot fish are found during summer with visibility of up to 10 metres. The sea bed is rocky with rocky off-shore reefs.

Spear-guns must have a gun licence, obtainable from the

police. The licence takes three weeks to obtain which rules out short-stay visitors. The licence also contains a list of regulations.

INDONESIA
Persatuan Olahraga Selam Indonesia, P.O.S.I., c/o., Fopindo JI., Prapatan 38, Jakarta

There is little information available, but the warm coral waters and many islands must make for first-class fishing.

REPUBLIC OF IRELAND
Irish Underwater Council, 3 AA Bty. Sarsfield, BKS, Limerick, Ireland

Although rough sea conditions are not uncommon, the west and south coasts offer good fishing for bass and large pollack in visibility averaging 10 metres and often reaching 25. Conditions and fish life are similar to west Devon and Cornwall. An Open Championship is held every year, usually at Valentia or Kilkee.

There are no restrictions, except that divers may not take shellfish or fish in freshwater.

ISRAEL
Federation for Underwater Activities in Israel, 37 Striker Street, Tel-Aviv, Israel

The Mediterranean coast does not appear very exciting from the spearfisherman's point of view, certainly not when compared to the Red Sea. The Israeli-controlled area around Eilat at the top of the Gulf of Aqaba is largely a nature reserve, although there are specific regions where fishing is permitted, but hardly encouraged. The best approach for the exciting fishing the Red Sea offers would be through Egypt or Saudi Arabia. The southern Saudi coast is good and would give access to the Farasan Islands, where a number of Italian groups have had spectacular diving and fishing, taking barracuda of 27 kilos. The changeable political situation in the countries bordering the Red Sea must be considered.

ITALY

Federazione Italiana Pesca Sportiva e Attività Subacquee, Viale Tiziano 70, 00100 Roma

The entire Italian coastline has favourable conditions for fishing but, as with France, experience is needed for the best results. The Adriatic side is better for the beginner with bass, bream and mullet. Sicily also requires specialist fishermen, but the Lipari and Aeolian Islands to the north are good with Filicudi and Alicudi best. The islands are reached by ferry from Naples or ferry or hydrofoil from Sicily.

Sardinia has also been heavily fished, but the southern part is still good; a liche of around 50 kilos was recently taken by Toschi, one of the top Italian fishermen.

To catch grouper in Italian waters requires experience and deep-diving ability.

No permits are required but one has to be over sixteen years of age. It is prohibited to:

Fish with an aqualung.
Fish within 500 metres of beaches used by bathers.
Fish within 50 metres of the external structures of ports or within 200 metres of fishing gear and anchored boats.

JAPAN

Japan Underwater Federation, G.P.O. Box 954, Tokyo, 100-91, Japan

The many islands around Japan ensure favourable conditions almost all the time, although access is a problem. Between July and October visibility reaches 20 metres. Grouper of 15 kilos have been taken in National Championships at Atami Shizuokaken and Japanese fishermen have performed well in international events.

A spearfishing permit is required and obtained from the local Federation of Professional Fishermen.

JAMAICA

Jamaica Sub-Aqua Club, P.O. Box 215, Mona Kingston 7, Jamaica, W.1.

There are perfect conditions all around the island with ample facilities throughout the year. Bonito, tuna, barracuda and wahoo are among the game fish found there.

KENYA

The Kenya Sub-Aqua Club, P.O. Box 49651, Nairobi, Kenya

The whole coastline offers tremendous fishing for a wide variety of fish, including parrot fish, bonito, tunny, wahoo and peacock fish. Michel Chanu, a Frenchman living at Malindi, has taken rock cod (grouper) of up to 6½ metres length, weighing 160 kilos.

Fishing is prohibited in the Marine National Parks at Malindi, Watamu in the central area, and Shimoni in the south, and a park is in the process of being established at Kiunga on the Somalia border in the north.

Underwater equipment is widely available for hire.

MALTA

Malta Sub-Aqua Club, 196 Vincent Bugeja Str. Hamrum

Taking everything into consideration, Malta has probably the most to offer in the Mediterranean. It is easily accessible; food, and car hire are reasonably priced and the fishing is good, especially in September and October, although the groupers tend to be in deep water. Conditions are good for most of the year. Visibility is very good, except in the Valletta area.

There are no restrictions, but a spear-gun licence must be obtained from the police.

MEXICO

Federacion Mexicana de actividades Subacuaticas, A.C., Puerta 9, Ciudad Deportiva Magdalena Maxhuca, Mexico 8, D.F.

With 9,212 kilometres of coastline, Mexico has vast opportunities and there are clear (except Mexican Gulf) warm waters with an average temperature of 25° C. Particularly favourable is from southern California southwards and the islands of the Caribbean coast with grouper, amberjack and large sea bass. Mexico's first competition was at Veracruz in 1958.

Permits can be obtained from the Department of Sports Fishing of the Ministry of Industry and Commerce, or through the Federation.

No fishing is allowed in the parks at Isla Mujeres, Cancun, Punta Nizuc, Veracruz, Puerto Vallarta, Cabo San Lucas and Guerro Negro.

MONACO

Club Chasse et Exploration Sous-marine de Monaco, 30 rue Grimaldi, Monaco

Monaco has similar conditions to the south of France with bass, bream and mullet being the main fish.

There are no regulations, but a permit is required.

MOROCCO

There are spearfishing clubs at Rabat, Casablanca, Tetuan, Kenitra and Agadir.

Mediterranean coast. Large grouper, ray running to over 200 kilos and all types of Mediterranean fish can be found. The best areas are Al Hociema, Ksar-es-Seghir, Qued Laou, Cape Ouilate and Cabo Negro. A boat is advisable to reach best fishing.

Atlantic coast. There is a great diversity of fish—mullet, sar, conger, liche and moray. It is particularly good for maigre. The water at Safi, Essaouira and Ifni is colder in summer than in winter; at Agadir, Rabat and Casablanca the reverse is true.

NEW ZEALAND

New Zealand Underwater Association, P.O. Box 875, Auckland, New Zealand

In New Zealand there is a wide variety of conditions and marine life—coral to kelp forest. Fishing is possible in the South Island during summer owing to sub-antarctic currents. The eastern coast of North Island offers best fishing, particularly the Bay of Plenty. The most sought-after fish are the kingfish (amberjack) and grouper, both of which attain large dimensions.

The Government has divided New Zealand waters into four categories, with various regulations. In the north, for example, six specimens per day are permitted. Local clubs can supply full details. There are weight and species limits in New Zealand's competitions.

NORWAY

Norges Dykkerforbund, Hauger, Skolevei 1 N-1351, Rud, Norway

Conditions are favourable throughout the country with variable visibility, the best time being June to August. The water is cold throughout the year. There are many fish familiar to British waters with good chances of large cod, coalfish and flat-fish.

There are no restrictions or regulations.

PANAMA

Club de Yates y Pesca, P.O. Box 4327, Panama 5, Panama

The Pacific coast has poor visibility except at the one hundred or more islands. On the Atlantic coast, the water is clear (particularly in October) and teems with big grouper, perch, barracuda, tarpon and others and would offer best possibilities.

PERU

Comision Nacional de Caza Submarina y Actividades Subacuaticas, Estadio Municipal, Tribuna Sur 3er, Casilla 2248, Lima, Peru

Peru has a rugged coast with many islands. The water is cold due to the Humboldt Current. Varieties of sars, cherlo, pintadilla, cagalo, ojo de uva, negro and various ray and flat-fish are available.

PORTUGAL

Federaçao Portuguesa de Actividades Subacuaticas, Rua do Arco do Cego, 90, 5°, Liseoa 1, Portugal

The entire Portuguese coastline offers favourable conditions. The area around Sesimbra and Cape St Vincent in the

Algarve in the south in particular. The western coast has rough seas in spring. The Azores, Madeira and Cape Verde Islands have clear, rich waters. There are bream and corvina and bass fishing is good. It is prohibited to:

Fish with an aqualung.
Fish within 50 metres of the beach.
Take more than two shellfish per day, to be taken by hand only.
Sell one's catch.
Use expellable gas weapons.

Fishermen must be over sixteen years old and if one stays longer than thirty days, a permit from the Maritime Delegation is required. Certain areas have prohibited zones and information should be sought from the local maritime authorities.

SINGAPORE

Singapore Underwater Federation, 279-M Selegie Complex, Singapore 7

Conditions are poor owing to pollution and low visibility, except around islands off the south coast. The east coast of Malaysia is good.

There are no regulations, except a spear-gun licence required in Malaysia.

SOUTH AFRICA

South African Underwater Union, P.O. Box 201, Rondebosh, 7700, Rep. of South Africa

The west coast is unsuitable. False Bay on the Cape itself is sheltered and offers marlin, tunny and yellow tail in summer with sea temperatures reaching 21° C. At Plattenberg Bay in February 1961, Tony Dicks a big fish specialist shot a 143-kilo black marlin. The fish was taken with a home-made CO_2 gun and towed Dicks for a mile before subdued. East London up to Natal offers good fishing, but little access in often rough seas. Natal is good but has strong currents and the heavy surf makes a boat useful. The sub-tropical waters north of Durban contain sharks and 600-kilo groupers. A spear-gun permit is required in Natal, issued by the Natal Parks Board. In the rest of the country you can shoot two non-pelagic (territorial dwelling) fish per day, weighing a minimum of 2.5 kilos. No fishing is allowed with an aqualung.

The coasts of Tanzania and Mozambique have large fish to offer, especially grouper and caranx. Favourable reports have come from Ibo and the French Comoro Islands in the north. Off the Mozambique coast, the island of Madagascar has much to offer with tuna, grouper and horse mackerel being a few of the many species abounding in the coral waters.

SPAIN

Federacion Espanola de Actividades Subacuaticas, Santaló 15, 3° 1a—Barcelona-21, Spain

The Atlantic coast of northern Spain and the Bay of Biscay have bream, bass and mullet. Good areas are San Sebastian and Santander. In the Mediterranean fishing is generally good in the less populated areas. Starting in the south, the British island of Gibraltar is a noted angling centre for large grouper, and spearfishermen have taken good fish despite the sheer cliffs and, in places, very deep water. Moving east along the Spanish coast areas of note are Malaga (off-shore reefs), Almeria and Cabo de Gata, the Cartagena peninsula. Of the Balearic Islands, Menorca and Ibiza are fair, whilst Majorca is disappointing unless one has local knowledge and good diving ability. The Canary Islands have, in the past, produced fine catches: grouper, bream, sea-perch and croaker, and the remote areas should still prove worthwhile. Like France and Italy, Spanish waters are fished by some of the world's best fishermen and whilst fish are available they are not easy to shoot. Spain is heavy on regulations. To fish in each region a permit must be obtained from the office of the local naval commandant. This is applied for on a form obtained from the office of the naval commandant, who will also issue a card to be signed by the applicant who must possess a medical certificate of diving fitness (see your own G.P. for this). In addition, one must hold a Federation Licence for the current year (valid for a year). All these documents can be obtained from the Spanish Federation or regional clubs and should be applied for at least a month in advance to avoid wasting fishing time on arrival.

Fishing with an aqualung is prohibited and it is an offence to have a gun and aqualung on a boat at the same time.

SRI LANKA (formerly Ceylon)

Sri Lanka has a thousand miles of coastline with good fishing for grouper, caranx, pompano, horse mackerel, mullet and barracuda on reefs from close in to a mile off-shore. The best fishing is around Colombo and down through Hikkaduwa. December through to March are the best months. Visibility of 50 metres is not uncommon in waters that reach over 80° F. Sharks are common.

Equipment can be hired and trips arranged at Colombo.

The world-record dog-tooth tuna (24 kilos) was taken off the south-east coast in 1959 by pioneer Sri Lankan fisherman, Rodney Jonklaas.

TRINIDAD AND TOBAGO

Over 300 species including fine game fish, such as kingfish, tuna (20 kilos), wahoo, pompano, snapper, crevalle jack and Nassau grouper are to be found. The islands are surrounded by coral reefs. There is a diving centre and resort at Bateaux Bay, Tobago.

TUNISIA

The Centre Nautique de Tunisie, 6 Place de la Monnaie, Tunis

The whole coastline teems with fish—mullet, grouper, ray and dogfish, for example. The islands of Djerba and Zembra, Raf-Raf, Zarzis and Korbous are good areas, with the best time being May to October.

The 1976 French National Championship was held at the small island of Galite in the north.

For details of regulations and permits required, apply to the above address.

TURKEY

Sualti Sporlari Federasyonu (Underwater Sports

Federation), Melek Han Kat 2, No. 18, Karaköy—Istanbul, Turquie

The Black Sea coast is unfavourable, but the Aegean and Mediterranean coasts offer good bass, mullet and bream. From Marmaris to Antalya and the remote islands are best. National and club competitions are held in which foreign fishermen are welcome to enter.

U.S.A.

Underwater Society of America, 732-50th Street, West Palm Beach, Florida, FL 33407, USA

Every conceivable type of fishing in sea, river and lake can be found in the U.S.A. Florida and California are obvious spots and Mexican California is also very good. Some of the world's best fishing is to be had around the oil rigs off New Orleans, from charter boats.

Regulations differ considerably from state to state, it is therefore necessary to obtain details from the local fish and game authorities.

VENEZUELA

Federacion Venezolana de Actividades Submarinas, Apartado Postal No. 58 356—Colinas de Bello Monte, Caracas, Venezuela

The entire Venezuelan coast offers good prospects. The coral areas have large grouper and barracuda.

YUGOSLAVIA

Savez za Sportski Ribolov na Mory i podvodne Aktivnosti FNR Jugoslavije, Rijeka Ul, Matije, Gupca 2

The entire coast and numerous islands offer good fishing for mainly small fish in shallow depths—mullet, bream and bass. On 29 December every year the Winter Cup of the Nations is held at Mali Losinj.

A permit is required and obtained from the local municipal office. The permit is valid throughout the area. In addition, there are often local restrictions on size of fish, catch limits and areas open for fishing. Local enquiries are a necessity.

Useful Translations

English	*French*	*Spanish*	*Italian*
Fins	Palmes	Aletas	Pinne
Fish	Poissons	Pesca	Pesce
Fish-keep	Accroche-Poissons	Pequeno Cable Porta Pesces	Cavetto portapesci
Float	Ballon	Boya	Boa
Gaff	Crochet	Rafio	Raffio
Gloves	Gants	Guantes	Guanti
Knife	Couteaux or Poignard	Cuchillos	Coltello
Mask	Masque	Mascara	Maschera
Net	Filet	Cinta	Rete
Reel	Moulinet	Carrate	Mulinello
Snorkel	Tuba	Respiradore	Aeratori
Spear	Flèche	Tridente	Arpón
Gun	Fusil	Fusile	Fucile
Rubber gun	Arbalète	Fucile elástica	Fucile Elastici
Compressed-air gun	Fusil pneumatique	Fucile pneumatico	Fucile pneumatici
Spring gun	Fusil à ressort	Fucile a resorte	Fucile a molla
Spearfisherman	Chasseur sous-marine	Pesca submarinista	Pescatore subacquea
Spearfishing	Chasse sous-marine	Pesca submarina	Pesca subacquea
Torch	Lampe	Linterna	Torcia
Watch	Montre	Reloj	Orologio
Weight-belt	Centre de lestage or Baudrier (harness type)	Cinturon de Lastre	Cintura zavorra
Wet suit	Vêtement	Trajes	Mute

Fish

In some countries certain fish have several names according to the locality—I list the most widely used.

English	*French*	*Spanish*	*Italian*
Atlantic and Mediterranean			
Bass	Loup	Lubina	Spigola
Grey Mullet	Mulet	Pardete	Cefalo
Pollack	Lieu jaune	Abadejo	Gado
Wrasse	Tanche	Tordo	Labride
Cod	Morue	Bacalo	Merluzzo
Mackerel	Maquereau	Caballa	Sgombro
Garfish	Aiguille	Aguja	Aguglia
Gurnard (Red)	Grondin	Arete	Cappone coccio
Red Mullet	Rouget de roche	Salmonete de roca	Triglia di scoglio
Bream (Black)	Griset	Chopa	Tanuta
Pouting	Capelan	Capellán	Merluzzo capellano
John Dory	Saint-Pierre	Pez de San Pedro	Pesce San Pietro
Plaice	Plie	Acedia	Passera
Sole	Sole	Lenguado	Sogliola
Turbot	Turbot	Rodaballo	Rombo
Brill	Barbue	Rémol	Rombo liscio
Flounder	Flet	Platija	Passera pianuzza
Ray (Thornback)	Raie bouclée	Raya de clavos	Razza chiodata
Electric Ray	Torpille	Tremielga	Torpedine
Sting-Ray	Raie pastenague	Pastinaca	Pastinacca
Angler	Baudroie	Rape	Rana pescatrice
Dogfish (Greater)	Grande rousette	Alitan	Gattopardo
Conger	Congre	Cóngrio	Grongo
Mediterranean			
Amberjack	Liche	Seriola	Leccia
Grouper[1]	Mérou	Mero	Cernia
Croaker	Corb	Corvina	Corvo

[1] The reader may be finding my alternating use of French and English names for certain fish in the text of this chapter confusing: e.g. *corb* not croaker on the one hand, and grouper not *mérou* on the other. The *liche* is rarely referred to as an amberjack, while many French and British fishermen call the golden bream (*oblade*) a gilthead. Britons use the Spanish/Italian *sargo* for the striped bream, or more often refer to all three as 'bream'. I have simply used the names most widely used among British fishermen.

Figure 29. Some principal Mediterranean fish: 1. Liche. 2. Grouper. 3. Dentex. 4. Corb. 5. Sar. 6. Moray.

English	*French*	*Spanish*	*Italian*
Dentex	Dente	Denton	Dentice
Moray	Murene	Morena	Murena
Bream (ringed)	Oblade	Oblada	Occhiata
Bream (striped)	Sar	Sargo	Sargo
Bream (golden)	Daurade	Dorada	Orata

9

CONCLUSION

For me, spearfishing is a kind of love-hate relationship.

The basic, simple satisfaction of obtaining meat through one's own efforts and skill—what greater pleasure is there than cleaning a fish in a sun-warmed pool at the end of a glorious day or as Bernard Gorsky put it: "mess about with fish on the pretext of cleaning and scaling them".[1] The feeling in the pit of the stomach of almost uncontrollable excitement when gazing out at unknown, crystal-clear reefs for the first time! The long swim back, laden with fish from those reefs, against the backcloth of an autumn sun setting behind tall, dark cliffs. That indescribable thrill as a large shape materializes from out of the gloom. Warm clothes and a flask of tea (albeit stewed) after a cold winter trip. The tension at a competition as figures slowly return from every direction at the end of the day; a few hours before some may have jostled for position on the end of a discharging sewer pipe (the famous, affectionately named 'Bunnies' at Southsea springs to mind) in a bizarre, silent comedy. The proud feeling of belonging to a world-wide brotherhood of men who actually shoot fish under the sea.

Against this there are the disappointments and frustrations. Long, fruitless journeys and the elusive, really big one that is lost at the end of a deep dive. The gruelling treadmill of swimming back against a strong, unrelenting tide with little reward and a mind full of missed chances. But there *is* "more to fishing than catching fish". Just being underwater, observing the sights and beauties, with the smell and feel of the sea, is in itself a unique experience. As you kick up from some shadowy recess, fingers groping feverishly for a hold in

[1] *Mediterranean Hunter* (Souvenir Press, 1954).

the gills of a bronze-flanked Cornish pollack, ascending faster and faster toward a silver ceiling, the disappointments and frustrations pale into insignificance. I suppose for most of us the initial and ensuing difficulties to overcome form a large part of the attraction; any feelings of regret over the killing of a beautiful, living creature being overshadowed by the magnificent, primitive art of its capture.

On a somewhat lighter note, you will, I am sure, be comforted to know that despite certain feelings against spearfishing mentioned earlier, the public at large seem to regard the catching of fish—whether with bent pin or speargun—as a perfectly natural, if not praiseworthy activity. The spearfisherman operating from a popular holiday beach need never be short of good sound advice and assistance. As he emerges from the depths, 'Dads' appear as if by magic, from behind crumbling sand-castles, towing small boys, eyes wide with amazement and admiration. Whilst the small boys exclamations are limited to "oohs" and "aahs", Dad is much more knowledgeable, informing the fisherman that the couple of mullet hanging from his belt are in fact cod or even salmon! As it would appear rude, if not cruel, to insist that the fish were mullet, the fisherman remains silent. The by-now thronging crowd is joined by a couple of little old ladies who proclaim the fisherman's heroism in "going down there", the more so without "oxygen bottles as used by *real* divers". They also wish to know if the fish are for breakfast or tea.

The fisherman, by now totally exhausted and in a state of severe dehydration, struggles along the beach, Pied Piper fashion; hordes of small boys muttering about sharks and fighting one another for the privilege of feeling the point of his 'harpoon'. All this and constant enquiries as to whether the fish are *really* dead. On occasion, if the fisherman is lucky, a suitably stout lad will suggest that he carries the fisherman's weight-belt or catch (preferably both). In the interests of adding another neophyte to the ranks this offer should never be refused, especially if steep cliffs or steps have to be endured before the sanctuary of car or anxious family is reached.

I hope my words have been of some help and encouragement

and that you too will experience what I firmly believe to be the world's finest sport—no, way of life! Good luck.

APPENDIX I: CLUBS

Confédération Mondiale des Activités Subaquatiques, 34 rue de Colisée, F-75008 Paris, France. C.M.A.S. is an International Federation linking the organizations of fifty-one countries.

The British Sub-Aqua Club, 70 Brompton Road, London, S.W.3., is the governing body of underwater sport in Britain with branches throughout the country. Some of these branches contain spearfishermen and stage national competitions. Four of the leading spearfishing branches are:

Southsea B.S-A.C. Spearfishing section: Adrian Worley, 7 Chadderton Gardens, Pembroke Park, Portsmouth, Hampshire.

Pontefract B.S-A.C., Mrs M. Hudson, 30 Baden Powell Crescent, Pontefract, Yorkshire.

Bournemouth and Poole B.S-A.C. Spearfishing section: Alan Stevens, 18 Petersham Rd., Creekmoor, Poole, Dorset.

Weymouth and Portland Associated Divers, Heather Harms, No. 6, Victoria Place, Easton, Portland, Dorset.

Specialist spearfishing clubs affiliated to the B.S-A.C.:

Exe Spearfishing Club, Sid Chamberlain, 22 Lincoln Close, Feniton, Devon.

Sussex Spearfishing Club, Mick Veal, 57 Cockmere Rd., Seaford, Sussex.

Any queries regarding spearfishing clubs should be addressed to: The Secretary, National Spearfishing Committee, B.S-A.C., 70 Brompton Rd., London S.W.3. or any of the above addresses.

The Sub-Aqua Association is an independent association of diving clubs with many branches throughout the country; concerned mainly with aqualung diving. Details from: S-A.A., 14 Private Road, Enfield, Middlesex.

Channel Islands

Guernsey. Blue Dolphin Sub-Aqua Club, Castle Emplacement, Guernsey, C.I.

Jersey. Jersey Sub-Aqua Club, La Folie, St Helier Harbour, St Helier, Jersey, C.I. Correspondence to: Beach Lodge, Roseville Street, St Helier.

International Underwater Hunters Federation

South African George Askew is in the process of forming a federation aimed mainly at protecting spearfishermen's interests. George, a correspondent for *Underwater World* can be reached at 82 Broadway Court, Broad Street, Durban 4001, South Africa.

APPENDIX II: RECORDS

Record Fish

The largest fish taken to date by a spearfisherman is a 364-kilo Jewfish (grouper). The fish was taken off Miami, Florida, USA by Don Pinder in 1955. Don, with his brother, Art, (who has even taken a sailfish) were great exponents of the Hawaiian sling, using it to take many large fish in the '50s.

The largest fish from our own waters is the 40.381-kilo angler taken by Jimmy Brown of Weymouth Associated Divers' Club. Jimmy took his fish at Chesil Cove, Portland, Dorset, in 1969.

British Spearfishing Records (excluding the Channel Isles) November 1979

	kg.	lb. ozs.	Captor	Date	Club
ANGLER (B)	40.381	80.9	J. Brown	1969	W.A.D.
BASS	8.706	19.3	C. House	1970	W.A.D.
BREAM—BLACK	1.588	3.8	E. Smith	1976	Sussex
BREAM—RAY'S	0.539	1.3	K. Matthews	1968	W.A.D.
BREAM—RED	1.163	2.9	A. Smith	1968	
BRILL (B)	3.984	8.13	M. Davies	1957	Brighton
COALFISH	2.590	6.335	A. Tostevin	1979	Jersey
COD	10.889	24.0	R. Milverton	1973	W.A.D.
CRAB (*)	4.764	10.8	D. Peake	—	Plymouth
CUTTLEFISH	2.155	4.12	W. Pack	1968	Sussex
DAB (B)	0.794	1.12	J. Burnside	1962	Plymouth
DOGFISH L/SPOTTED (B)	1.418	3.2	P. Crawford	1972	Exe

	kg.	lb. ozs.	Captor	Date	Club
DOGFISH G/SPOTTED (B)	7.146	15.12	B. Lamont	1973	S/Sea Bubbles
EEL—CONGER	25.404	56.0	E. Smith	1976	Sussex
EEL—SILVER	1.730	3.13	M. Bradshaw	1972	Sussex
FLOUNDER (B)	1.814	4.0	J. Lowe	1979	Bournemouth
GARFISH	0.596	1.5	C. House	1966	W.A.D.
GURNARD—RED (B)	1.163	2.9	D. Way	1972	Plymouth
JOHN DORY	2.651	5.14	R. Price	1969	Bournemouth
LOBSTER (*)	5.445	12.0	F. Vincent-Hunt	1968	Bristol
MACKEREL	0.751	1.11	G. Savidge	1970	Salcombe
MONKFISH (B)	22.062	48.10	J. Weeden	1968	Sussex
MULLET—GREY	3.404	7.8	G. Upton	1960	Plymouth
MULLET—GOLDEN	0.820	1.808	D. Bartlett	1979	S/Sea Bubbles
MULLET—RED	1.248	2.12	A. Worley	1972	Southsea
OCTOPUS (*)	3.403	7.8	M. Aldridge	1960	Brighton
PLAICE (B)	3.273	7.2	K. Hearn	1967	Aldershot
POLLACK	7.484	16.8	M. Bradshaw	1976	Sussex
POUT WHITING	1.162	2.9	R. Pyle	1971	Sussex
POUTING	0.907	2.0	B. Evans	1971	Sussex
RAY—BLONDE (B)	12.591	27.12	F. Drake	1959	Plymouth
RAY—CUCKOO (B)	2.666	5.14	A. Worley	1972	Southsea
RAY—ELECTRIC (B)	29.265	64.8	D. Taylor	1966	Plymouth
RAY—PAINTED (B)	4.980	11.0	P. Beard	1976	Southsea
RAY—SPOTTED (B)	3.460	7.10	E. Byrne	1972	Sussex
RAY—STING (B)	27.223	60.0	R. Brooker	1967	Sussex
RAY—THORNBACK (B)	11.343	25.0	P. Smith	1968	Plymouth
ROCKLING 3-BEARDED (B)	0.751	1.11	B. Carlson	1971	Plymouth
SALMON (*)	6.806	15.0	M. House	1966	W.A.D.
SCAD	0.454	1.0	S. Smiley	1967	Plymouth
SEA SCORPION L.S. (B)	0.897	1.15	R. King	1971	Pontefract
SEA TROUT (*)	2.908	4.10	R. Pyle	1971	Sussex
SHARK—BLUE	10.889	24.0	D. Canniford	1955	Plymouth
SHARK—SMOOTH HOUND	1.928	4.4	P. Crawford	1970	Plymouth
SKATE—COMMON (B)	16.334	36.0	T. Hall	1960	Weymouth
SOLE (B)	1.843	4.1	E. Smith	1976	Sussex
SQUID (*)	1.361	3.0	J. Hendy	1959	Plymouth
SUN FISH (*)	8.470	18.11	C. Latham	1976	Bournemouth
TRIGGER-FISH	1.500	3.5	B. Lamont	1973	S/Sea Bubbles
TURBOT (B)	11.343	25.0	W. Dagger	1959	W.A.D.
WEAVER—GREATER (B)	0.454	1.0	P. Crawford	1971	Exe
WRASSE	3.630	8.0	A. Down	1965	Plymouth

(B) Denotes designated flat- or bottom fish.
(*) Denotes fish that the N.S.F.C. recommend be excluded from competitions.

World Breath-Held Diving Records

I include a list of breath-held depth records and a number of timed dives as a point of academic interest. With a couple of exceptions, all the depth records were established by spearfishermen. I trust the reader will take careful note of Chapter 4 and in no way try emulate these feats. An attempt on Jacques Mayol's present depth record—even by an experienced man—could very easily prove fatal.

DEPTH RECORDS

Name	*Depth (Metres)*	*Location*	*Date*
Raimondo Bucher	30	Naples, Italy	November 1949
Ennio Falco and Alberto Novelli	35	Naples, Italy	December 1951
Raimondo Bucher	39	Capri, Italy	November 1952
Ennio Falco and Alberto Novelli	41	Rapallo, Italy	1956
Americo Santarelli	43	Rio de Janeiro, Brazil	1960
Americo Santarelli	44	Circeo, Italy	September 1960
Enzo Maiorca	45	Syracuse, Italy	September 1960
Americo Santarelli	46	S. Margherita, Italy	October 1960
Enzo Maiorca	49	Syracuse, Italy	October 1960
Enzo Maiorca	50	Syracuse, Italy	August 1961
Enzo Maiorca	51	Ustica, Italy	August 1962
Enzo Maiorca	53	Syracuse, Italy	August 1964
Enzo Maiorca	54	Acireale, Italy	July 1965
Tetake Williams	59	Rarotonga, Polynesia	September 1965
Jacques Mayol	60.3	Freeport, Bahamas	June 1966
Enzo Maiorca	62	Syracuse, Italy	November 1966
Robert Croft	64.6	Fort Lauderdale, USA	February 1967
Enzo Maiorca	64	Cuba	September 1967

(Also at Cuba in 1967, Italian, Guiliana Trelcani, set the present women's record of 44.97.)

Robert Croft	66.2	Fort Lauderdale, USA	December 1967
Jacques Mayol	70.4	Fort Lauderdale, USA	January 1968
Robert Croft	73.1	Fort Lauderdale, USA	August 1968
Enzo Maiorca	72	Ognina, Italy	August 1969
Enzo Maiorca	74	Ognina, Italy	August 1970
Jacques Mayol	75	Futo, Japan	September 1970
Jacques Mayol	76	Ito, Japan	September 1970
Enzo Maiorca	77	Ognina, Italy	August 1971
Enzo Maiorca	78	Ognina, Italy	August 1972
Enzo Maiorca	80	Genoa, Italy	August 1973
Jacques Mayol	85	Elba, Italy	November 1973
Jacques Mayol	86	Elba, Italy	November 1973
Enzo Maiorca	87	Sorrento, Italy	September 1974
Jacques Mayol*	92	Elba, Italy	October 1975

* An advocate of yoga, the 50-year-old Mayol took 3 minutes 39 seconds for this dive. It is particularly interesting when one compares it with the 133-metre world record for a dive with compressed air (aqualung) by the Americans, Gruener and Watson in the Bahamas in 1968.

DURATION

There is, of course, a vast difference in duration between a 'working' dive—such as during a competition—and simply sitting still on the bottom of a swimming pool. Mayol, in collaboration with Cressi-sub is currently working on the physiology of endurance in breath-held diving.

1 minute	The Ama, diving girls of Japan, do around fifty 1-minute dives a day in search of shellfish and edible seaweed.
1 minute 20 seconds to 1 minute 40 seconds	*Consistent* times by Chilean Raoul Choque during the 1971 World Championship. American John Ernst did 1 minute 25 seconds to 1 minute 30 seconds (timed by Colin Mcleod).
2 minutes	The Italian team during the 1969 World Championship.
2 minutes 7 seconds	Anthony Paheroo, a Tahitian member of the French Team at the above competition (both timed by Mayol).
2 minutes 30 seconds	Sixty-year-old Arab sponge-diver during a dive to 77 metres at Djerba Island, Tunisia. Witnessed by Cousteau in 1939.
2 minutes 35 seconds	The average time by Tahitian divers, worked out by a consul, J. Lamb Doty.
2 minutes 40 seconds	A pearl-diver at Hikuera in the Tuamotus Islands, South Pacific, October 1968, during a dive to 30.9 metres.
3 minutes	A woman at Anaa Atoll in the Tuamotus during a dive to 45.5 metres.
3 minutes 14 seconds	Jean Medina, during the 1954 World Championship.
4 minutes 45 seconds	A diver in the Tuamotus (timed by a B. Merwin). Divers of the French Oceanic Establishment, motionless in shallow water.

7 minutes	Personal claim by Hadjistathis, a Greek sponge-diver in 1913. He is known to have reached 77 metres and claimed he could reach 110.
13 minutes 42.5 seconds	World record by Californian, Robert Foster. He hyperventilated with oxygen for 30 minutes prior to sitting on the bottom of a San Rafael swimming pool in 1959. (*Guinness Book of Records*).

APPENDIX III: EQUIPMENT AGENTS

In case you have difficulty in obtaining some of the equipment mentioned in Chapter 2, I list the British main agents.

BEUCHAT. Submarine Products Ltd., Hexham, Northumberland.

CRESSI and SPORASUB. International Diving and Watersports, 1 New Road, Shoreham-by-Sea, Sussex.

CHAMPION. Unfortunately no agent at present but equipment available on the Continent.

G.S.D. Guns. Namron (Aqua Products) Ltd., 264 Newhall Road, Sheffield, Yorkshire.

G.S.D. Masks, snorkels, fins, torches. Spartan, A. Tillbrook & Co. Ltd., Delamere Road, Cheshunt, Hertfordshire.

MARES. Blandford Sub-Aqua, 13 Langham Garden, Wembley, Middlesex.

NEMROD. Wisden Edwards, Pershore Trading Estate, Pershore, Worcestershire.

PIRELLI-ULIXES. Collins & Chambers Ltd., 197–201 Mare Street, London E.8.

SPIROTECHNIQUE/TECHNISUB. Spirotechnique Ltd., Silverdale Road, Hayes, Middlesex.

TURNBULL. Hannimex Ltd., Hannimex House, Faraday Road, Swindon, Wiltshire.

Sandford & Down, 24 Pier Street, West Hoe, Plymouth, Devon carry a good selection of specialized spearfishing equipment.

APPENDIX IV: BIBLIOGRAPHY

Sources of reference for this work

The Underwater Naturalist, Pierre De Latil, Jarrolds, 1954.
Man and the Underwater World, Pierre De Latil and Jean Rivoire, Jarrolds, 1956.
The World Beneath the Waves, Dr Gilbert Doukan, Allen & Unwin, 1957.
Skin Diver Magazine, Los Angeles, California, U.S.A.
Triton formerly *Neptune*, journal of the B.S-A.C. (now renamed *Diver*).
Apnea a Meno Cento, Jacques Mayol, Fratelli Fabri, Milan, 1976.
The National Geographic Magazine, Washington D.C., U.S.A.
International Yearbook of the Underwater World (C.M.A.S.), Editions Aquatica, Lausanne. 3rd. Edition, 1974–5, 4th Edition, 1978–9.
Mediterranean Seafood, Alan Davidson, Penguin Books, 1972.
The Observer's Book of Sea Fishes, T. B. Bagenal, Frederick Warne, 1972.

Further reading

The books listed below are, with one exception, not concerned with fishing in British waters and although some of the instructional works are now outdated they are still of interest to spearfishermen.

Underwater Hunting, Dr Gilbert Doukan, Allen & Unwin, 1953. French instructional classic.
Moana; Moana Returns, Bernard Gorsky, Elek, 1956. 2 vols. Worldwide interest.
Mediterranean Hunter, Bernard Gorsky, Souvenir Press, 1954. Another French instructional classic.
Hunting Big Fish, Marcel Isy-Schwart, Burke, 1954. France and the Mediterranean, Haiti, Brazil.
Shark Hunters, Ben Cropp, Macmillan, 1971. Australia.
My Adventure Under the Sea, Jean Foucher-Créteau, Muller, 1957. France, Canaries, Red Sea and Cape Verde Islands.
Spearfishing in Britain, Kendall Macdonald and Phil Smith, Stanley Paul, 1963. Instructional.

Sub-Marine Spearfishing, Vane Ivanović, Kaye, 1951. Instructional.
Modern Spearfishing, Vane Ivanović Kaye, 1954. Revised edition, Kaye & Ward, 1974. Instructional.
The Blue Continent, Folco Quilici, Weidenfeld & Nicolson, 1954. Red Sea.
Dahlak, Gianni Roghi and Francesco Baschieri, Nicholas Kaye, 1956. Red Sea.
Lord of the Sharks, Franco Prosperi, Hutchinson, 1955. Sri Lanka.
Undersea Hunting for Inexperienced Englishmen, James Aldridge, Allen & Unwin, 1955. Instructional.
Guide to Underwater Hunting, Simon Codrington, Adlard Coles, 1954. Instructional.
La Chasse Sous-Marine, Tony Salvatori (in French), Société Oceans, Marseille, France. Authoritative instructional.
The Super Snorkellers, David Way, *Sub-Aqua* Magazine, May 1976. History of depth records.

Periodicals

Mondo Sommerso. An Italian magazine containing magnificent colour photography, much spearfishing coverage and international competition reports.
Etudes et Sports Sous-Marines. Excellent French magazine that gives full coverage of international competitions and spearfishing in general.
L'aventure Sous-Marine (in French). General diving interest.

The above three magazines can be obtained on subscription through leading newsagents such as W. H. Smith or Willens of London.

Underwater World (British). Frequently contains spearfishing news and articles. Available from newsagents and dive shops.
Sub-aqua Scene. Official magazine of the Sub-Aqua Association. Available from newsagents and dive shops.
Skin Diver (American). Available from dive shops and some larger newsagents.
Diver. Official journal of the B.S-A.C. Sent to all members and available from dive shops.

NOTES ON UNDERWATER PHOTOGRAPHS

The underwater photographs in this book were taken in available light with a Nikonos camera. Plates 14, 25, and the jacket, High Speed Ektachrome (400 ASA). Plates 11, 12 and 13, Fujicolor F-11 (100 ASA). Depths: 5 metres (4 metres visibility) and maximum 9 metres (11 metres visibility) respectively.

INDEX

Numbers in italics denote pages on which figures appear